SHAPED BEADWORK & BEYOND

Dimensional Jewelry in Peyote Stitch

Diane Fitzgerald

LARK JEWELRY & BEADING

LARK JEWELRY & BEADING

An Imprint of Sterling Publishing
387 Park Avenue South
New York, NY 10016

ISBN 978-1-4547-0909-1

Distributed in Canada by Sterling Publishing
c/o Canadian Manda Group, 165 Dufferin Street
Toronto, Ontario, Canada M6K 3H6
Distributed in the United Kingdom by GMC Distribution Services
Castle Place, 166 High Street, Lewes, East Sussex, England BN7 1XU
Distributed in Australia by Capricorn Link (Australia) Pty. Ltd.
P.O. Box 704, Windsor, NSW 2756, Australia

For information about custom editions, special sales, and premium and corporate purchases, please contact
Sterling Special Sales at 800-805-5489 or specialsales@sterlingpublishing.com.

Email academic@larkbooks.com for information about desk and examination copies.
The complete policy can be found at larkcrafts.com.

Every effort has been made to ensure that all the information in this book is accurate. However, due to differing
conditions, tools, and individual skills, the publisher cannot be responsible for any injuries, losses, and other
damages that may result from the use of the information in this book.

Manufactured in China

2   4   6   8   10   9   7   5   3   1

larkcrafts.com

SHAPED BEADWORK & BEYOND

CONTENTS

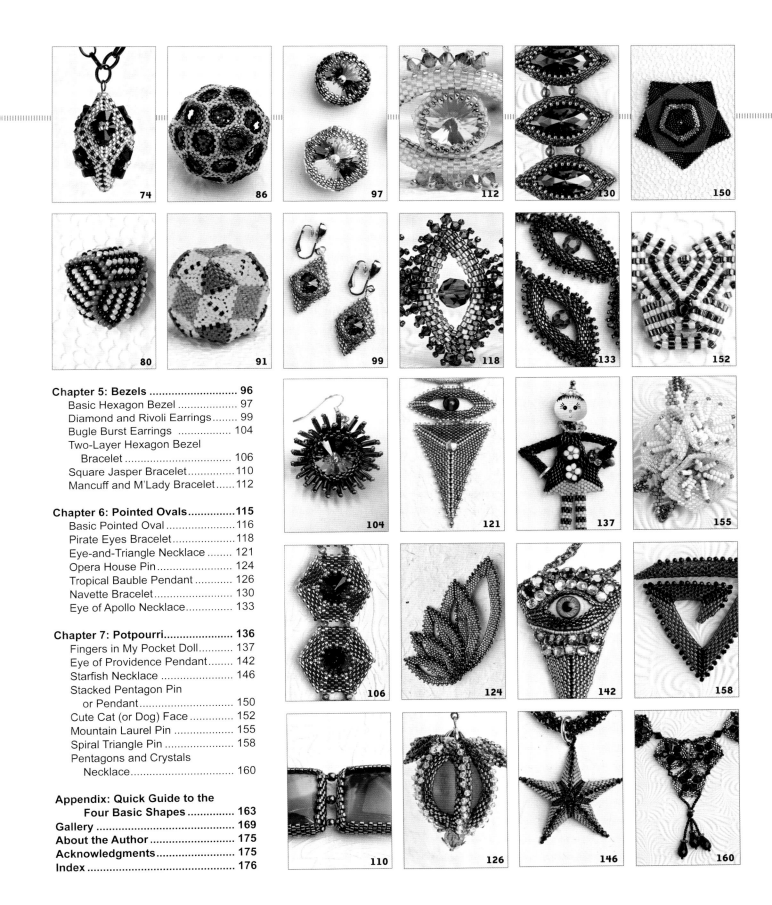

INTRODUCTION

Photo by Claire Bischoff

SHAPE IS A UNIVERSAL DESIGN element in jewelry. It vies with color and sparkle in importance and spurs our imagination because we associate shapes with ideas. Through symbolism, shapes give us clues to the meaning and significance of adornment. Triangles may suggest movement and direction, for example, while the square denotes stability and grids.

This book takes shapes in exciting new directions in both their geometric and their natural forms. If you enjoyed my earlier book, *Diane Fitzgerald's Shaped Beadwork*, which shows how to create amazing dimensional jewelry with peyote stitch using four basic shapes, you'll see that *Shaped Beadwork & Beyond* takes it to the next level with patterned shapes, the use of crystals, and a whole slew of fascinating new three-dimensional shapes. At the same time, this book stands on its own because I explain how to make the most basic building blocks for all the projects. Although these may appear complex, the careful instructions and illustrations will make it easy to create any of the pieces in the book.

If you haven't worked with shapes before, you may wish to begin by making the Basic Triangle described on page 17. Then, as shown in the instructions that follow it, combine it with more triangles to create stars, spherical Temari Beads, and even a darling cat face! After learning the teardrop shape on page 47, you can go on to make a simple Heart Pin, butterflies, or an Art Deco-inspired pendant. You can join basic squares into a Pillow Bead, a bezel, or when combined with triangles, Moorish Tile Beads.

Warning: It might be hard to choose among the forty-plus patterns offered in this book! And as if that wasn't enough selection, almost every project includes variations.

With only simple supplies—beads, needle, and nylon thread—you can create jewelry that's fun to make and that you'll cherish for a lifetime.

This book is designed as a reference you can turn to again and again for ideas and inspiration. I hope the projects encourage you to take them in new directions and help you imagine wonderful new pieces that are all your own.

Diane M. Fitzgerald

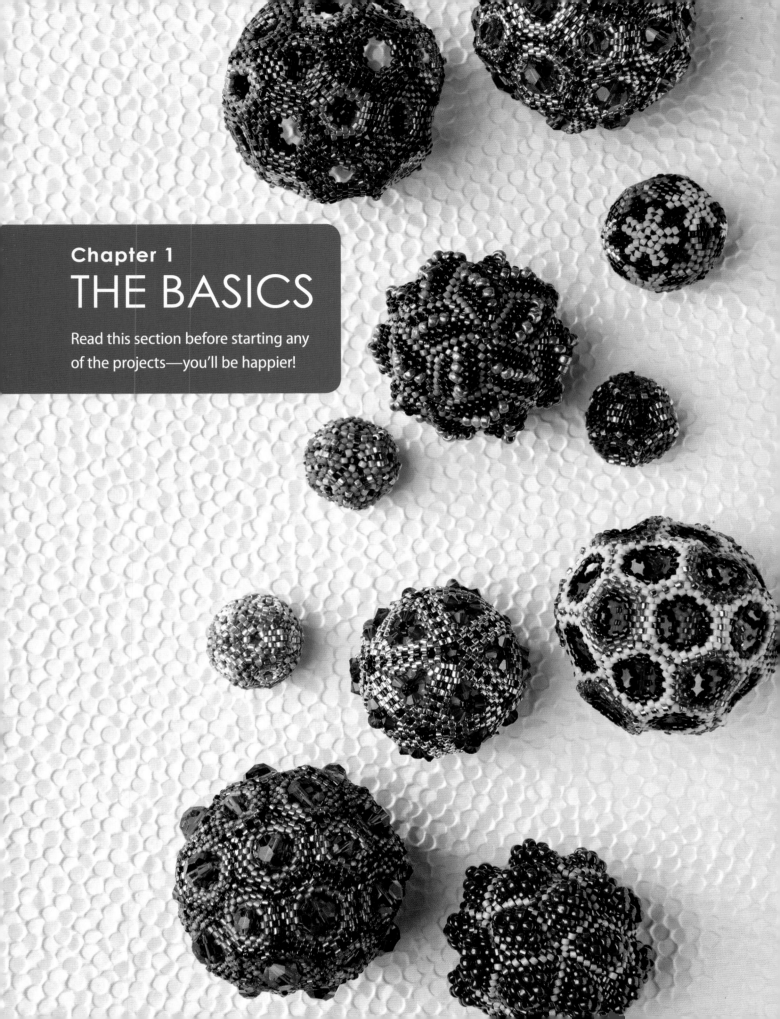

Chapter 1
THE BASICS

Read this section before starting any of the projects—you'll be happier!

Basic Beadwork Kit

Here's a list of the supplies and tools I store in a plastic pencil box, with helpful descriptions.

Thread

- Nymo D on a bobbin in several colors
- FireLine 6 lb in smoke and crystal

I use FireLine for its durability when stitching with crystals. Because of the extensive color selection, I use Nymo for everything else.

Beading Needles, Sizes 10 and 12

Keep your needles safe in a wood needle case—beaded, of course—or look for a small Evening in Paris perfume bottle in antique stores. The cobalt blue glass and slight whiff of 70-year-old perfume is always a delight.

Scissors

- Kid's Fiskars for cutting FireLine
- Small sharp scissors for cutting Nymo

Wax

I prefer microcrystalline wax—the slightly tacky kind that comes in a cup and stays that way for years. Use it to prevent fraying, remove twist, and help two strands of thread adhere to each other.

Top to bottom: a knot remover, a thread picker, and a ruler

Disposable Lighter

For melting the ends of threads after I've knotted and clipped them, my favorite tool is an economical disposable lighter. (See Preparing the Thread on page 13 for more details.)

Pen or Pencil

Ruler and Tape Measure

Choose the kind with both inches and centimeters.

Knot Remover

A knot remover is a type of curved tweezers with sharp points. To use it, hold the knot on the tip of your forefinger, squeeze the points of the tweezers together, then plunge the points into the heart of the knot and let the points expand. Repeat until the knot begins to loosen.

Thread Picker

This little tool is handy when you need to loosen a thread or pull out work. Here's how to make one: Select a large flat bead for the handle. Wrap the eye end of a size 20 needlepoint needle with thread until it fits snugly in the hole of the bead. Squirt white glue on the thread and into the bead hole, then insert the wrapped end of the needle into the bead. Let dry.

Needle Puller

Keep a short piece of a wide rubber band on hand to help you grab a needle and pull it through a tight bead.

Peyote Stitch

Peyote stitch, the primary technique used throughout this book, is perhaps the oldest and most widely used method for weaving beads together. It's considered an off-loom stitch because no loom is required. As new beads are added to previous rows, you simply hold the work in your hand.

Understand the Technique

Peyote stitch begins with either a string of beads for flat peyote stitch or a ring of beads for circular peyote stitch as row 1. Circular peyote patterns in this book require a step up at the end of each row in order to be in position to begin the new row. (For counting purposes, the first row becomes both the first and the second rows as the stitching progresses.) When adding a bead (by skipping a bead and passing through the next bead), the new bead pushes the skipped bead down. Adding beads this way is how the characteristic "up" and "down" bead pattern occurs.

To begin peyote stitch, string the number of beads needed for the first row. Add one bead (the first bead on the new row) and pass through the second bead on the previous row, counting from where the thread exits a bead. Continue to add one bead and pass through the second bead across the row or along the ring (**figure 1**).

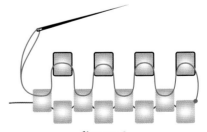

figure 1

One peyote stitch consists of adding one bead and passing through the second bead along the previous row.

The instructions in this book proceed counterclockwise for circular peyote stitch. (Lefties work clockwise.)

Circular Peyote Step Up

To begin a new row when working in even-count circular peyote, you must pass through two beads at the end of the row—the last bead of the previous row and the first bead added in the current row. Another way to describe a step up is to pass through two beads before beginning a new row—the bead that completes the last stitch and the next bead. In **figure 2** the two beads with bold outlines are the step-up beads.

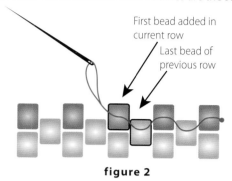

First bead added in current row

Last bead of previous row

figure 2

On most patterns, the step up moves one bead to the left with each new row. This can be confusing when a corner increase and the step up both occur at the same corner. When this happens, pass through the bead in the previous row (this completes the row), and then pass through the first of the increase beads.

If you have trouble keeping track of the step up, count out the number of increase beads for each row. When you've used them all, the step up should be along the next side. For example, if you're making a pentagon and the row requires adding three beads at each corner, then count out five piles with three beads in each one.

Beginning a new row in the middle of a side can also be confusing. For example, if the pattern says peyote five times on each side, you may need to add the first two beads of the row before you reach the corner. You'll add the remaining three beads for that side at the end of the row.

Zip Edges with Connector Beads

To join two peyote stitch edges with matching "up" beads, work an extra row of peyote on either edge. These newly added beads become the connector beads. Align the pieces so the connector beads on one edge fit between the "up" beads on the other edge. Zip the edges together by weaving back and forth between beads (**figure 3**).

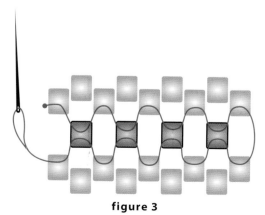

figure 3

General Techniques

Essential Knots

Three knots are handy for beadwork. The overhand knot (also called a half-hitch knot) is used at the end of new thread (**figure 4**). The square knot ties two threads together (**figure 5**). Use the lark's head or sales tag knot to secure the beginning ring of beads (**figure 6**).

Overhand Knot

Holding the thread in your left hand with the end of the thread in your right hand, pass the end of the thread over the part in your left hand. Then pass the end through the loop just formed.

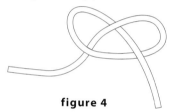

figure 4

Square Knot

Pass the left thread over the right thread and around it. Then pass the right thread over the left thread and through the loop.

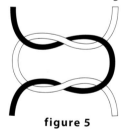

figure 5

Lark's Head Knot

Form a ring of beads secured with a lark's head knot. (See Forming a Ring of Beads, page 13.)

figure 6

Preparing the Thread

I recommend working with doubled thread for durability. With the required length of thread in the needle, bring the ends together and slide the needle to the middle. Wax the thread with micro-crystalline wax, starting at the needle end. Tie the ends together with an overhand knot.

Melting the Thread Tails

To avoid weaving in thread tails, whether I'm working with Nymo or Fire-Line, here's my technique:

After knotting the thread, clip the tails about 1 mm from the knot. Hold the thread between the thumb and forefinger of your left hand with the ends of the thread extending about ¼ inch (6 mm) beyond your fingertips.

Using your right hand, ignite a disposable lighter with the side of your thumb and hold down the switch. (A lighter makes a tinier knot than a thread burner and is much cheaper.) Hold the lighter straight up. Brace the middle and ring fingers of your left hand against the lighter to steady your hand.

Slowly extend your thumb and forefinger toward the flame so that the thread ends are *near* the base of the flame, not in it (**figure 7**). When they have melted slightly, withdraw the thread. *Don't let the thread catch on fire.* Test the knot by pulling apart the strands.

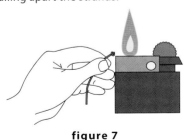

figure 7

Forming a Ring of Beads

When I begin a piece of beadwork with a ring of beads, I use a lark's head or sales tag knot to eliminate weaving in a pair of tails later. Prepare the thread as described above, then string the required number of beads and slide them to within 1 inch (2.5 cm) of the knot. Separate the strands between the beads and the knot. Pass the needle between the strands, tighten the thread to form a ring, and pass back through the last bead strung. Don't allow the knot to slip into a bead (**figure 6**).

Adding Thread

Although there are many methods of adding thread, this is what I suggest: Leave the current thread attached to indicate where to join the new thread. Prepare a new thread as described above and tie an overhand knot on one end of the thread, leaving the other end slightly longer. Pass through six beads, working toward the bead where your old thread is exiting. Allow the knot to catch inside a bead. Then, weave in the old thread and clip (**figure 8**). After working a few stitches, clip the exposed end of the new thread.

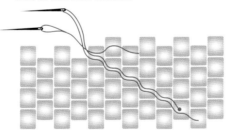

figure 8

Positioning Beads

As you sew beads in place, it's important to position each one correctly. When adding a single bead, make sure that it sits with its hole parallel to the bead in the row below. If two beads are added as a corner increase, they should sit with their holes parallel and almost perpendicular to the other beads in the row. Make sure the thread is not twisted at their base.

Undoing Stitches

We all make mistakes, but don't compound a mistake by passing the point of the needle back through a bead. You're likely to pierce a thread in the process. Instead, gently *pull* (don't push) the eye of the needle back through the bead, wiggling it a little if necessary.

Adding Three Beads at a Corner

When working squares or pentagons, some rows require adding three beads at each corner. The middle bead of the three must be down or recessed because on the next row, two beads will sit in the valley just created. You can sometimes position the center bead by pulling the outer beads outward with your needle, pushing down on the center bead with your fingernail, and then tightening the thread.

Here's another way to ensure that the center bead is recessed: Add the first two of the three increase beads at a corner, then pass back through the corner bead in the row below. Pass forward through the second bead of the two just added, then add the third bead and continue through the next bead (**figure 9**). (This method was shown to me by a dear little old Japanese lady who spoke no English, and we all thank her for it!)

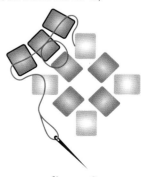

figure 9

Stitching in the Ditch

Stitching in the ditch, a term borrowed from quilters, means sewing along a seam line. In beading it means adding beads on top of a completed row of peyote stitch. To stitch in the ditch, exit a bead, add a bead, and, skipping the bead below, pass through the next bead on the row (**figure 10**).

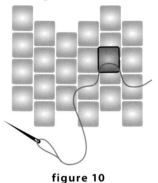

figure 10

Stiffening the Beadwork

Some beadwork may need a little starch to help it hold its shape, especially if you plan to string it. If a beaded bead collapses or compresses, it can leave an unsightly gap along the strand.

Two brands of acrylic floor polish work well for stiffening beadwork, Pledge with Future Finish (formerly Future Acrylic Floor Polish) and Mop & Glo. I keep some in a small jar, which is convenient for dipping beaded shapes into the liquid. After dipping, let the excess drip off and allow the piece to dry on waxed paper, rolling it a few times every 5 to 10 seconds to prevent the liquid from draining out.

Stringing Beaded Beads

SUPPLIES

Nymo D or FireLine 6 lb

Size 10 beading needle

G-S Hypo Cement

Heavy nylon cord (Conso #18)

Scissors

2 clamshell bead tips

Clasp

1 Make a thread harness to pull the nylon cord through beaded beads as shown in **figure 11**. Thread your needle with 8 inches (20.5 cm) of Nymo D or FireLine. Tie the ends together with a square knot (don't use an overhand knot), glue the knot, and let dry.

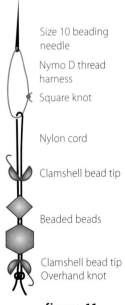

Size 10 beading needle

Nymo D thread harness

Square knot

Nylon cord

Clamshell bead tip

Beaded beads

Clamshell bead tip
Overhand knot

figure 11

2 Cut a piece of nylon cord twice the desired length of the finished necklace plus 8 inches (20.5 cm). Pass the cord through the thread harness and knot the ends with an overhand knot. Clip the ends close to the knot, apply glue, and let dry.

3 String a bead tip, pulling the knot into the clamshell, and then string your beaded beads.

4 To finish, string the second bead tip, exiting the open end of the clamshell. Cut the nylon cord near the thread harness. Tie a square knot so that it fits tightly inside the bead tip and there are no gaps between the beads. When making the second half of the knot, pass through the loop a second time (this forms a surgeon's knot). Glue the knot and let dry. Clip the ends and close the bead tip.

5 Attach one side of the clasp to each bead tip.

Recognizing the Patterns

Each of the four basic shapes—triangles, squares, pentagons, and hexagons—used in this book has a unique pattern of increases at each corner. (The sides are peyote stitch without increases.) Learning to recognize the pattern for each shape helps prevent mistakes and makes counting rows easier.

In the figures below, increase beads are shown in gray, while side beads are white.

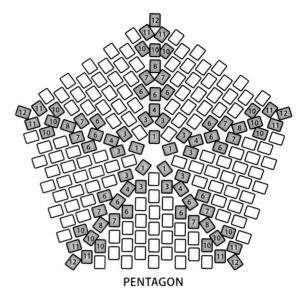

PENTAGON

Beginning with row 6, the increase pattern repeats itself from rows 6–9. The pattern for adding beads at the corners is 3, 2, 1, 0. (Zero means no beads are added in that row; you pass through the single corner bead in the previous row.)

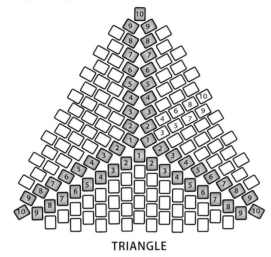

TRIANGLE

Two beads are added at each of the three corners on every row. On the last row, add either a pair of beads or a single bead (as shown on row 10). The triangle increase pattern is the simplest of the four basic shapes.

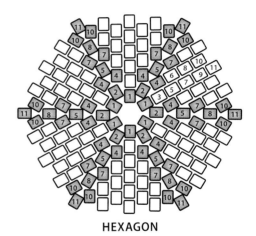

HEXAGON

Beginning with row 4, the increase pattern repeats itself from rows 4–6. The pattern for adding beads at the corners is 2, 1, 0. (Zero means no beads are added in that row; you pass through the single corner bead in the previous row.)

SQUARE

The increase pattern repeats itself from rows 3–7. The pattern for adding beads at the corners is 3, 2, 2, 1, 0. (Zero means no beads are added in that row; you pass through the single corner bead in the previous row.)

Chapter 2
TRIANGLES

The triangle is the simplest of the basic shapes covered in this book. In this chapter, we'll explore how to combine triangles to form spheres, stars, and other shapes.

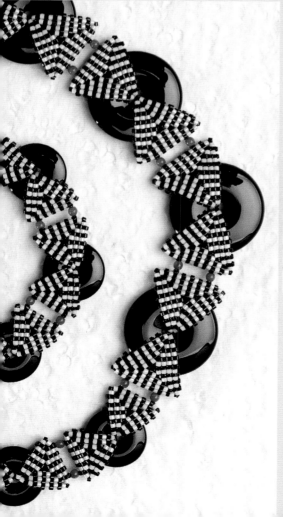

SUPPLIES

Size 11° cylinder beads:

   27 A (shown in light gray)

   18 B (shown in dark gray)

Nymo D or FireLine 6 lb

Size 10 beading needle

Microcrystalline wax

Scissors

Lighter

BASIC TRIANGLE

If you don't know how to stitch a basic triangle, practice using this pattern first.

With 1 yard (about 1 m) of thread in your needle, bring the ends together, wax well, knot, clip the tail close to the knot, and melt the ends slightly.

Note: In the diagrams below, new beads are shown with a bold outline.

Row 1: String 3 As and form a ring secured with a lark's head knot as follows: Push the beads to within 1 inch (2.5 cm) of the knot. Separate the strands between the beads and the knot. Pass the needle between the strands, tighten, then pass back through the last bead strung (**figures 1** and **2**). Don't allow the knot to slip into a bead. Orient the work so you're working counterclockwise (lefties, work clockwise).

figure 1

figure 2

Row 2: *Add 2 Bs and pass through the next A. Repeat from * two more times. Step up (**figure 3**).

figure 3

Note: These beads form the three corners of the triangle. Make sure the pairs of beads at each corner sit almost parallel to each other. Adjust them if necessary.

Row 3: *Add 2 As and pass through the next B. Add 1 A, skip one bead in the row below, and pass through the next B. Repeat from * two more times. Step up (**figure 4**).

figure 4

Row 4: *Add 2 Bs and pass through the next A. Peyote twice with B. Repeat from * two more times. Step up (**figure 5**).

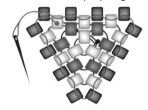

figure 5

Row 5: *Add 2 As and pass through the next B. Peyote 3 with A. Repeat from * two more times. Step up (**figure 6**).

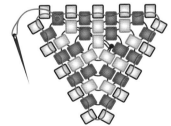

figure 6

SUPPLIES

Size 11° cylinder beads:

A (shown in yellow), 15 g

B (shown in dark gray), 15 g

13 black 5-mm round faceted beads

1 hook-and-eye clasp

1 head pin

4 eye pins

Nymo D or FireLine 6 lb

Size 10 beading needle

Microcrystalline wax

Scissors

Lighter

Round-nose pliers

Wire cutters

DIMENSIONS

18 inches (45.5 cm) long

OH MY STARS! NECKLACE

As it encircles your neckline, this necklace sparkles and shimmers like the stars in the night sky. The concentric circles in each star are formed when the striped triangles are connected. For a shimmering holographic effect, use gold iris cylinder beads. For a sparkling effect, work with cut cylinders in silver.

Overview

For the stars in this necklace, join five triangles to form a slightly domed pentagon (**figure 1**). Then add one triangle to each side of the pentagon to create the star's points (**figure 2**).

figure 1

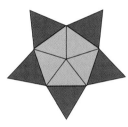

figure 2

Pentagon

Make the first five-row triangle following the Basic Triangle instructions on page 17. Add connector beads to the first triangle as follows: Stitch a single B at each corner and peyote with B along all three sides. Weave in the thread and clip (**figure 3**).

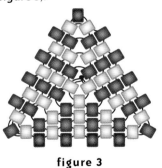

figure 3

Make a second five-row triangle. Add connector beads to the second triangle as follows: Stitch a single B at each corner and peyote with B along only two sides. Don't peyote along the third side (**figure 4**). Leave the thread attached to zip this triangle to the first.

figure 4

Align the B beads on any side of the first triangle so they fit between A beads on the side of the second triangle without connector beads. With your thread exiting an A on the second triangle, pass through the A on the first triangle. Pass through the A on the second triangle again in a circular fashion (**figure 5**).

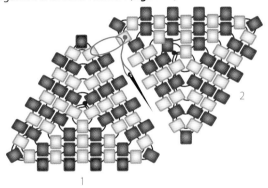

figure 5

Continue to weave back and forth between the first and second triangles, zipping them together. After exiting the last A on the second triangle, pass through the opposite A on the first triangle again (**figure 6**). Weave in the thread and clip.

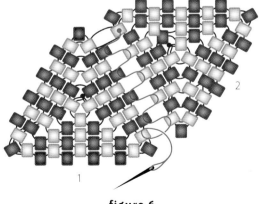

figure 6

Make and join the third and fourth five-row triangles as for the second triangle.

To add the fifth five-row triangle, add 1 B and pass through the next A at this corner. Peyote along one side with B. Add 1 B and pass through the next A at this corner. Then pass through the opposite A on the fourth triangle as shown in **figure 5**.

Pass through the A bead just exited on the fifth triangle again, then zip the edges together, working toward the center. At the inner corner of the fifth triangle, add 1 B and pass through the next A (**figure 7**).

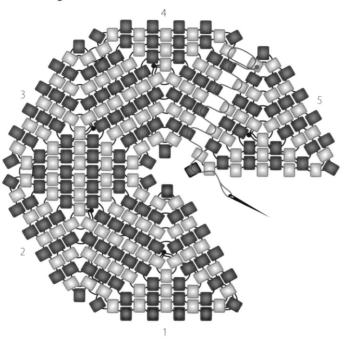

figure 7

Pass through the opposite A on the first triangle, working toward the center. Pass counterclockwise through the 5 Bs at the center, then pass through the A where your thread exited on the fifth triangle (**figure 8**).

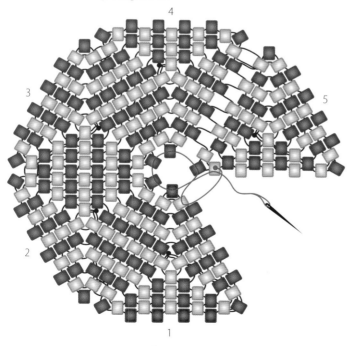

figure 8

Continue zipping the fifth triangle to the first triangle to form a pentagon. Weave in the thread and clip.

Note: After adding the fifth triangle, the piece will be slightly domed (**figure 9**). There should be four "up" B beads on each side plus the corner beads.

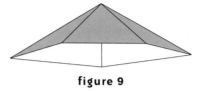

figure 9

Add Star Points

Make another five-row triangle. Add B beads at three corners and peyote along two sides with B. Join the triangle to one side of the pentagon as shown in **figures 5** and **6**. Weave in the tail and clip.

Repeat to add triangles to the remaining four sides of the domed pentagon (**figure 10**).

Make a total of seven stars.

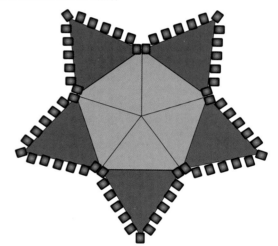

figure 10

Assemble

Prepare your thread as for the Basic Triangle. Anchor the thread so it exits a B at the tip of a star. Add one 5-mm round bead and pass through a B at the tip of the next star. Pass back and forth through the tip beads and the 5-mm round bead until the beads are filled with thread (**figure 11**). Weave in the thread and clip. Repeat to connect all seven stars.

figure 11

Adjustable Clasp

Anchor a new thread so it exits a B at the tip of the last star. Add one 5-mm round bead and the hook-and-eye clasp. Pass back and forth between the B, the clasp, and the 5-mm round bead as in **figure 11** until the beads are filled with thread. Weave in the thread and clip.

On the opposite end of the necklace, make a chain with round beads as follows:

String a 5-mm bead onto a head pin, clip the head pin 3⁄8 inch (1 cm) from the bead, and form a simple loop. Repeat, using the four eye pins. Before closing each loop, attach it to the loop on the previous bead.

Weave your remaining thread through beads so it exits a B at the tip of the last star. Add one 5-mm round bead and pass back and forth between the

B and the loop of the last eye pin in the chain, passing through the 5-mm round bead as in **figure 11** until the beads are filled with thread. Weave in the thread and clip.

Variation with Graduated Stars

Single Star with Loop

Single Star with Crystal Fringe

SUPPLIES

Size 11° cylinder beads:

  A (dark gray), 11 g

  B (light gray), 13 g

16 round 5-mm faceted beads

1 head pin

5 eye pins

1 hook-and-eye clasp

Nymo D or FireLine 6 lb

Size 10 beading needle

Microcrystalline wax

Scissors

Lighter

Round-nose pliers

Wire cutters

DIMENSIONS

20¼ inches (51.5 cm) long

Make one large, four medium, and four small stars, varying the size of the basic triangle by working the following number of rows:

Large triangle—7 rows (not including connector beads)

Medium triangles—5 rows

Small triangles—3 rows

TEMARI BEADS

SUPPLIES FOR ONE BEAD

Size 11° cylinder beads:

  A (shown in dark gray), 2 g

  B (shown in yellow), 2 g

Nymo D or FireLine 6 lb

Size 10 beading needle

Microcrystalline wax

Scissors

Lighter

DIMENSIONS

Each bead: 1¼ inches (3.2 cm)
in diameter

The drawing on this photo shows how a completed triangle fits into the structure of the ball.

The exquisite wrapped-silk designs of Japanese temari balls inspired these beaded beads. Originally, temari balls were popular Japanese toys, but over time they evolved into a traditional art form.

My Temari Beads are hollow and consist of 20 triangles joined to form a spherical shape known as an icosahedron. After completing a basic bead, consider adding patterns within each triangle. For inspiration, look on the Internet or at books about temari balls for color and design ideas.

Basic Bead

To make the bead larger or smaller, increase or decrease the number of rows in each triangle.

1 Following the directions for the pentagon and star points on pages 19 and 20, make one star with four-row triangles instead of five-row triangles. This forms half of a Temari Bead.

2 Make a second star the same as the first, but don't add connector beads to the outside edges or outside corners. Add only the single bead at the two corners nearest the pentagon (**figure 1**). Don't cut the thread.

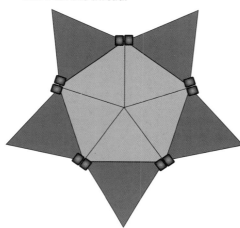

figure 1

Note: The connector beads that join the second star to the first are already in place on the first star. Add the third corner bead when zipping the two stars together.

3 Invert the second star so that its points face downward and place the first star on it with its points upward. The outer tips of the second star will fit in the valley between two triangles on the first star (**figure 2**). Using the remaining thread from the second star, zip the two stars together so the triangles mesh (**figure 3**).

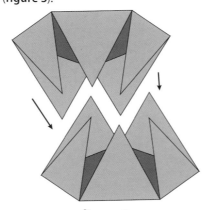

figure 2

figure 3

When doing so, add a single B at these corners, pass through the next A, then weave through the five connector beads as shown in figures 7 and 8 for the Oh My Stars! Necklace on page 20. Weave in the thread and clip.

Note: If it's necessary to stiffen your bead, dip the finished piece in clear acrylic floor polish and let it dry on waxed paper. Roll it a few times to prevent the floor polish from draining out.

Necklace

These are the patterns for the beads in the necklace, numbered counterclockwise from the upper left, as shown in **figure 4**. Each bead requires approximately 3 grams of cylinder beads.

In the figures below, A represents black beads and B is the contrast color. Reverse the colors for interesting effects.

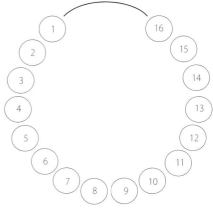

figure 4

Bead 1

Polka Dots, figure 5

Row	Corners	Sides
Row 1:	3B	-
Row 2:	BB	-
Row 3:	BB	B
Row 4:	BB	B, B

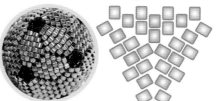

figure 5

Connector beads are B, B, B on the sides; outer corner beads are A.

Bead 2

Dots and Dashes, figure 6

Row	Corners	Sides
Row 1:	3A	-
Row 2:	AA	-
Row 3:	AA	B
Row 4:	BB	A, A

figure 6

Connector beads are A, B, A on the sides; outer corner beads are B.

Bead 3

Bead 3 has a random design, so the pattern is not included.

Bead 4

Stars and Dots, figure 7

Row	Corners	Sides
Row 1:	3A	-
Row 2:	BB	-
Row 3:	BB	A
Row 4:	BB	A, A

figure 7

Connector beads are B, A, B on the sides; outer corner beads are B.

Bead 5

Lotus Petals, figure 8

Row	Corners	Sides
Row 1:	3B	-
Row 2:	BA	-
Row 3:	BA	A
Row 4:	BA	A, A

figure 8

Connector beads are A, A, A on the sides; outer corner beads are B.

Bead 6

Concentric Pentagons, figure 9

Row	Corners	Sides
Row 1:	3A	-
Row 2:	BB	-
Row 3:	AA	A
Row 4:	BB	B, B

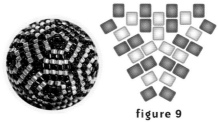

figure 9

Connector beads and corner beads continue the color pattern.

Bead 7

Turk's Head Knot, figure 10

This pattern results in a sphere that appears to have interwoven bands similar to triaxial weaving.

Row	Corners	Sides
Row 1:	3A	-
Row 2:	AB	-
Row 3:	AA	B
Row 4:	AB	A, B

figure 10

Connector beads continue the color pattern B, A, B; corner beads are A. This pattern requires that the basic triangles have an even number of rows. Be careful to match the stripes as you assemble the bead.

Bead 8

The Web, figure 11

Row	Corners	Sides
Row 1:	3A	-
Row 2:	BB	-
Row 3:	BB	A
Row 4:	BB	B, B

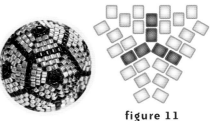

figure 11

Connector beads are A, B, A; corner beads are A.

Bead 9

Diamonds, figure 12

Row	Corners	Sides
Row 1:	3A	-
Row 2:	AA	-
Row 3:	AA	B
Row 4:	AA	B, B

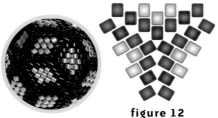

figure 12

Connector beads are B, B, B on the sides; corner beads are A.

Bead 10

Stars, figure 13

Row	Corners	Sides
Row 1:	3A	-
Row 2:	BB	-
Row 3:	BB	A
Row 4:	BB	A, A

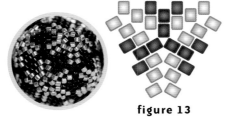

figure 13

Connector beads are B, B, B on the sides; corner beads are B.

Bead 11

Pentagon Outline Pattern, figure 14

Row	Corners	Sides
Row 1:	3B	-
Row 2:	AA	-
Row 3:	AA	B
Row 4:	AA	A, A

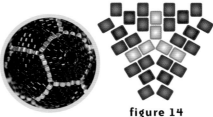

figure 14

Connector beads are A, B, A on the sides; corner beads are A.

Bead 12

Diamond Flower Pattern, figure 15

Row	Corners	Sides
Row 1:	3A	-
Row 2:	AB	-
Row 3:	AB	B
Row 4:	AB	B, B

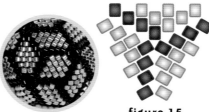

figure 15

Connector beads are B, B, B on the sides, corner beads are A.

Bead 13

Random Triangles, figure 16

Row	Corners	Sides
Row 1:	AAB	-
Row 2:	AA, AB, BA	-
Row 3:	AA	A
	AB	B
	BA	A
Row 4:	AA	A, A
	AB	B, B
	BA	A, A

figure 16

Connector beads are A, A, A on the sides; corner beads are A. Assemble the triangles randomly and reverse the colors on some triangles if you wish.

Bead 14

Daisies, figure 17

Row	Corners	Sides
Row 1:	3B	-
Row 2:	BB	-
Row 3:	BB	A
Row 4:	BB	A, A

figure 17

Connector beads are B, B, B on the sides; corner beads are A.

Bead 15

Spinner, figure 18

Row	Corners	Sides
Row 1:	3A	-
Row 2:	AB	-
Row 3:	AB	A
Row 4:	AB	B, B

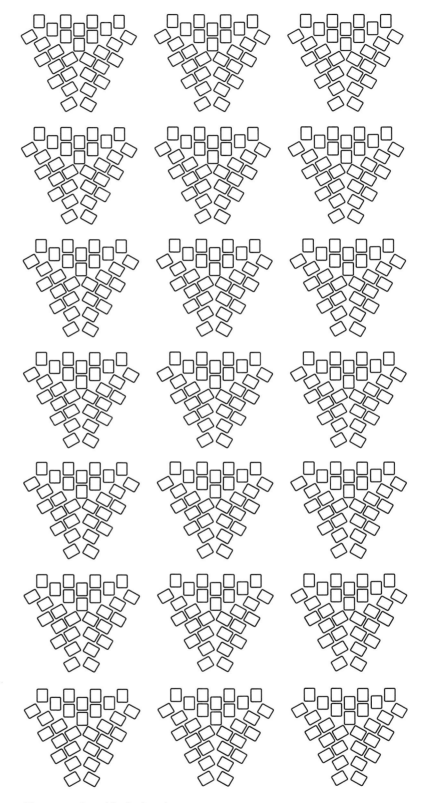

figure 18

Connector beads are B, A, B on the sides; corner beads are A.

Bead 16

Stitches, figure 19

Row	Corners	Sides
Row 1:	3B	-
Row 2:	BB	-
Row 3:	BB	A
Row 4:	BB	A, A

figure 19

Connector beads are A, A, A on the sides; corner beads are A.

See page 14 for information on stringing the beads into a necklace.

Photocopy these blank triangles to create your own Temari Bead designs.

Variation

Another color combination that works well is using silver-lined beads in bright colors for A through F and gold for row 1, the side beads, and the connector beads. In this example the triangles have five rows instead of four and the bead is slightly larger. See page 28 for more infomation.

Variation with Multicolored Stars

The drawing on this photo shows how a completed triangle fits into the structure of the ball.

This bead calls for six accent colors (A through F) plus the background color (shown here in black). Each triangle is a four-row version of the Basic Triangle on page 17 with "spokes" of increase beads that form each corner (**figure 20**).

Each triangle calls for a specific set of colors (**figure 21**).

Note: Use black for all row 1 beads and for the side and connector beads. The single corner bead at the end of each spoke matches the color of that spoke.

Begin by making and connecting five triangles to form

the center pentagon, as for the basic bead on page 24. Starting with the triangle in the upper left of the center pentagon, make the spokes using colors A, E, and D. Working clockwise, make the second triangle using A, D, and C; the third triangle using A, C, and B; the fourth using A, B, and F; and the fifth using A, F, and E.

Continue following the pattern shown in **figure 21** to make and join 20 triangles. Check off the triangles as you make and attach each one.

figure 20

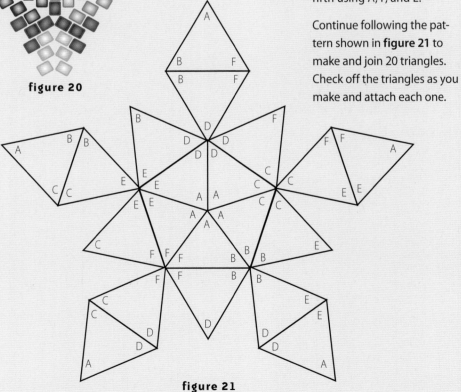

figure 21

SUPPLIES

Size 11° cylinder beads:

  A (shown in dark gray), 3 g

  B (shown in yellow), 3 g

Felt, 4 x 4 inches (10 x 10 cm)

**2 shank buttons, ⅜ inch (1 cm)
in diameter**

**Purchased tassel, 1½ inches
(3.8 cm) long**

1 black 4-mm round crystal

Nymo D or FireLine 6 lb

Size 10 beading needle

Microcrystalline wax

Scissors

Lighter

DIMENSIONS

1½ inches (3.8 cm) in diameter;
¼ inch (6 mm) deep

CHEVRON PENDANT

Like the other beads in this chapter, the chevron stripe is a
variation of the color pattern used in the Basic Triangle.

First Hexagon— First Triangle

With 1½ yards (about 1.5 m) of thread in your needle, bring the ends together, wax well, knot, clip the tail close to the knot, and melt the ends slightly.

Row 1: String 3 As and form a ring secured with a lark's head knot as follows: Push the beads to within 1 inch (2.5 cm) of the knot. Separate the strands between the beads and the knot. Pass the needle between the strands, tighten, then pass back through the last bead strung (**figures 1** and **2**). Don't allow the knot to slip into a bead. Orient the work so you're working counterclockwise (lefties, work clockwise).

figure 1

figure 2

Row 2: *Add 1 A and 1 B and pass through the next A. Repeat from * two more times. Step up (**figure 3**).

figure 3

Note: These beads form the three corners of the triangle. Make sure the pairs of beads at each corner sit almost parallel to each other. Adjust them if necessary.

Row 3: *Add 2 As and pass through the next B. Add 1 B, skip one bead in the previous row, and pass through the next A. Repeat from * two more times. Step up (**figure 4**).

figure 4

Row 4: *Add 1 A and 1 B and pass through the next A. Peyote once with A and once with B. Repeat from * two more times. Step up (**figure 5**).

figure 5

Row 5: *Add 2 As and pass through the next B. Peyote the side with B, A, and B. Repeat from * two more times. Step up (**figure 6**).

figure 6

Row 6: *Add 1 A and 1 B and pass through the next A. Peyote the side with A, B, A, and B. Repeat from * two more times. Step up (**figure 7**).

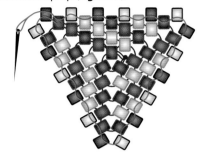

figure 7

Row 7: *Add 1 A and pass through the next B. Peyote the side with B, A, B, A, and B. Repeat from * two more times. These are the connector beads for the first triangle. Weave in the thread and clip (**figure 8**).

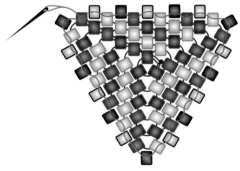

figure 8

First Hexagon—-Second Triangle

Follow along with **figure 9**. Make the second triangle as for rows 1–6 of the first triangle. Add 1 A and pass through the next A. Zip the next side of this triangle to one side of the previous triangle, aligning the beads to form the chevron pattern.

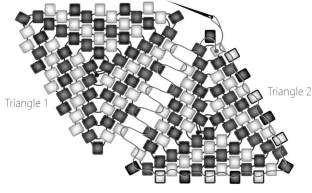

figure 9

Add connector beads to the two remaining corners and sides of the second triangle as follows: *Add 1 A and pass through the next A. Peyote along the side with B, A, B, A, and B. Repeat from * once. Weave in the thread and clip.

First Hexagon—Third, Fourth, and Fifth Triangles

Make and join the third, fourth, and fifth triangles as for the second triangle.

First Hexagon—Sixth Triangle

Note: The connector beads are already in place on the first and fifth triangles, so they only need to be added to the outer edge of the sixth triangle.

Follow along with **figure 10**. Make the sixth triangle as for rows 1–6 of the first triangle. Add 1 A at the corner, then peyote the outer edge with B, A, B, A, and B. Add 1 A

at the next corner, then zip the next side of the sixth triangle to the side of the first triangle. Add 1 A and pass through the next A in the sixth triangle.

Pass through the opposite bead in the fifth triangle, then continue to zip the last side of the sixth triangle to the side of the fifth triangle. Weave in the thread and clip.

Second Hexagon

Repeat the steps above to make a second hexagon of triangles, but don't add connector beads to the outer edge of the triangles.

Assemble

Cut two or three hexagons from the felt, making them slightly smaller than the beaded hexagons. Place the felt between the beaded hexagons as padding.

Zip the outer edges of the beaded hexagons together, passing through each group of four corner beads in a circle to reinforce it. Anchor your thread and pass through the six corner beads at the center, then sew one button to the center on each side. Sew the tassel to the bottom and add a loop of beads or bail to the top connected with the round crystal.

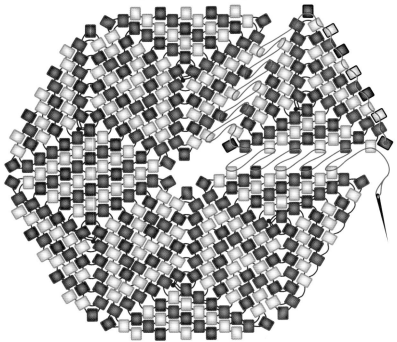

figure 10

SUPPLIES

Size 11° cylinder beads:

A (shown in light gray), 4 g

B (shown in dark gray), 2 g

60 red 4-mm bicone crystals (Swarovski 5328)

FireLine 6 lb

Size 10 beading needle

Microcrystalline wax

Scissors

Lighter

DIMENSIONS

1½ inches (3.8 cm) in diameter

The drawing on this photo shows how a completed triangle fits into the structure of the ball.

CRYSTALS AND TRIANGLES BALL

You'll make the Crystals and Triangles Ball by following the steps for the Temari Beads on page 24, but add crystals to the centers of each triangle in row 2.

With 2 yards (about 2 m) of thread in your needle, bring the ends together, wax well, knot, clip the tail close to the knot, and melt the ends slightly.

Row 1: String 3 Bs and form a ring secured with a lark's head knot as follows: Push the beads to within 1 inch (2.5 cm) of the knot. Separate the strands between the beads and the knot. Pass the needle between the strands, tighten, then pass back through the last bead strung (**figures 1** and **2**). Don't allow the knot to slip into a bead. Orient the work so you're working counterclockwise (lefties, work clockwise).

figure 1

figure 2

Row 2: *Add 1 crystal and 2 As. Pass back through the crystal, then pass through the next bead on the ring. Repeat from * two more times. Step up through the crystal and the first A (**figure 3**).

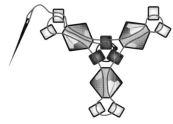

figure 3

Row 3: *Add 2 As and pass through the next A. String 5 As and pass through the first A at the next corner. Repeat from * two more times. Step up (**figure 4**).

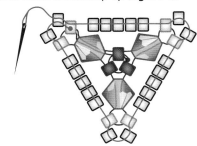

figure 4

Row 4: *Add 2 As and pass through the next A. Peyote 4 with A. Repeat from * two more times. Step up (**figure 5**).

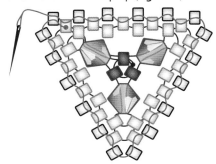

figure 5

Assemble this bead following the pattern for the Temari Bead shown in figure 2 on page 24.

Variation

SUPPLIES

Size 11° cylinder beads:

A (shown in teal), 2 g

B (shown in brown), 2 g

Size 11° seed beads:

C (shown in gray), 2 g

Size 8° seed beads:

D (shown in green), 2 g

Nymo D or FireLine 6 lb

Size 10 beading needle

Microcrystalline wax

Scissors

Lighter

DIMENSIONS

1¾ inches (4.5 cm) in diameter

The drawing on this photo shows how a completed triangle fits into the structure of the ball.

BUMPY ICOSA BEAD

Substitute size 11° and size 8° seed beads for some of the cylinders in a Temari Bead and you get a completely different look. You'll stitch these Bumpy Icosa Beads following the steps for the Temari Beads, but you'll make six-row triangles instead of four-row triangles.

With 2 yards (about 2 m) of thread in your needle, bring the ends together, wax well, knot, clip the tail close to the knot, and melt the ends slightly.

Row 1: String 3 As and form a ring secured with a lark's head knot as follows: Push the beads to within 1 inch (2.5 cm) of the knot. Separate the strands between the beads and the knot. Pass the needle between the strands, tighten, then pass back through the last bead strung (**figures 1** and **2**). Don't allow the knot to slip into a bead. Orient the work so you're working counterclockwise (lefties, work clockwise).

figure 1

figure 2

Row 2: *Add 1 A and 1 B and pass through the next A. Repeat from * two more times. Step up (**figure 3**).

figure 3

Row 3: *Add 1 A and 1 B and pass through the next B. Add 1 C, skip one bead in the row below, and pass through the next A. Repeat from * two more times. Step up (**figure 4**).

figure 4

Note: Keep the tension tight so the size 8° beads pop out.

Row 4: *Add 1 A and 1 B and pass through the next B. Peyote twice with C. Repeat from * two more times. Step up (**figure 5**).

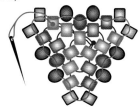

figure 5

Row 5: *Add 1 A and 1 B and pass through the next B. Peyote once with D and twice with C. Repeat from * two more times. Step up (**figure 6**).

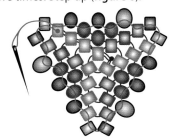

figure 6

Assemble this bead following the pattern for the Temari Bead shown in figure 2 on page 24.

Row 6: *Add 1 A and 1 B and pass through the next B. Peyote 1 with C, 1 with D and twice with C. Repeat from the *two more times. Step up.

Assembly: See Temari Beads. For connector beads add 1 A and pass through the next B at the corner; on the sides add C, D, C, C.

Note: When adding connector beads, make sure the lines of size 8° beads form a diagonal. If necessary, flip the triangle over so the lines match.

Variation

This version of the Bumpy Icosa Bead uses a slightly different pattern, as shown in **figure 7** and in the chart below.

Row	Corners	Sides
Row 1:	3A*	-
Row 2:	AB	-
Row 3:	AB	C
Row 4:	AB	C, C
Row 5:	AB	C, D, C
Row 6:	AB	C, D, D, C

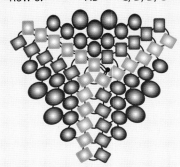

figure 7

* These beads form the beginning ring.

Connector beads are C, D, D, D, C; corner beads are A.

Variation

Beaded by Carmian Seifert

BICYCLE CHAIN NECKLACE AND BRACELET

In this high-contrast set, black onyx donuts are connected with black-and-white striped triangles accented with bright red beads.

Overview

The necklace consists of 14 large, double-sided triangles that connect the large onyx donuts and eight small triangles that connect the small onyx donuts. The triangles share a single corner bead that connects them through the hole of the donut, and they're zipped together along the top edge.

Large Triangle—Front

With 2 yards (about 2 m) of thread in your needle, bring the ends together, wax well, knot, clip the tail close to the knot, and melt the ends slightly.

Rows 1–8: Make the front side of the large triangle following the instructions for the Basic Triangle on page 17, but work eight rows instead of five. Begin with B for row 1 and all odd-numbered rows. Work all even-numbered rows with A (**figure 1**). Make 14 triangle fronts.

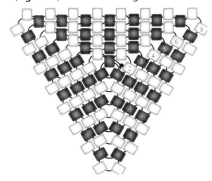

figure 1

Row 9: *Add 1 B and pass through the next A. Peyote 7 with B. Repeat from * two more times. Weave in the thread and clip (**figure 2**).

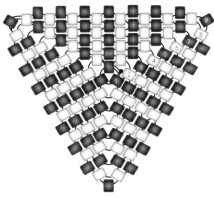

figure 2

Large Triangle—Back

Make 14 triangle backs following the directions for rows 1–8 above, then assemble the triangles as described below.

Assemble the Triangles

Pass through the next A at the corner where you just stepped up, but don't add a bead (**figure 3**). Peyote along the first edge of the back triangle with B. At the corner, pass through the hole of a large donut, pass through the single bead added in row 9 of the front triangle, then pass back through the donut and the next A at the corner of the back triangle.

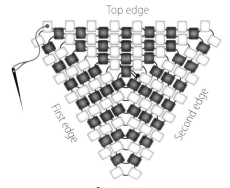

figure 3

Peyote along the second edge of the back triangle with B and pass through the single corner bead on the front triangle. Zip the top edge of the back triangle to the top edge of the front triangle. Pass through the single corner bead on the front triangle and the first A on the back triangle (**figure 4**).

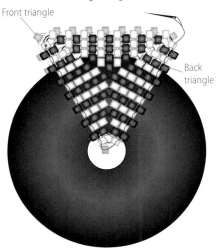

figure 4

Necklace

SUPPLIES

Size 11° cylinder beads:

   A (shown in white), 15 g

   B (shown in black), 15 g

7 black 30-mm onyx donuts

4 black 20-mm onyx donuts

24 red 3-mm round opaque beads

1 two-strand fold-over clasp, ¾ inch (2 cm) wide

Nymo D or FireLine 6 lb

Size 10 beading needle

Microcrystalline wax

Scissors

Lighter

DIMENSIONS

19 inches (48.5 cm)

Note: For a longer necklace, add two 20-mm donuts and 3 grams of each color of cylinder beads. You can also extend the length by adding more 3-mm beads before attaching the clasp.

Bracelet

SUPPLIES

Size 11° cylinder beads:

   A (shown in white), 7 g

   B (shown in black), 7 g

6 black 20-mm onyx donuts

10 red 3-mm round opaque beads

**1 two-strand fold-over clasp,
¾ inch (2 cm) wide**

Nymo D or FireLine 6 lb

Size 10 beading needle

Microcrystalline wax

Scissors

Lighter

DIMENSIONS

8¼ inches (21 cm)

Make 12 small triangle fronts and 12 small triangle backs as for the necklace. Connect these to the donuts and then to each other using 3-mm beads.

Attach half the clasp to each end. Weave in any remaining threads and clip.

Weave in the thread and clip on the first triangle only. On the remaining triangles, don't clip the thread.

Attach a second front and back triangle to the first donut the same way. Repeat to assemble all the front and back triangles into seven units.

Note: A donut with two pairs of front and back triangles attached will now be called a "unit." As you connect triangle fronts and backs around a donut, use the same thread to join one unit to the next.

Connect the Large Units

Align two units as shown in **figure 5**.

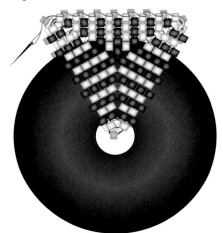

figure 5

Pass through beads along the top edge so the thread exits the third B from the left. Add one 3-mm round bead. Pass through the corresponding bead on the opposite unit. Pass back and forth

through these beads again to reinforce the join (**figure 6**).

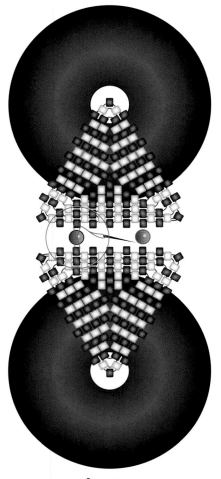

figure 6

Small Triangle Units

Make eight small front triangles with seven rows each (work the seventh row the same as row 9, above) and eight small back triangles with six rows each. Assemble the small triangles into four units as described above using the small donuts.

Attach the small units to each other between the second Bs on the top edges, using 3-mm beads. Join the small units to the large units by stitching the second B on the small unit's top edge to the third B bead on the large unit's top edge.

Add the Clasp

Attach half the clasp to each end using 3-mm beads. Weave in any remaining threads and clip.

SUPPLIES

Size 11° cylinder beads:

A (accent beads, shown in brown), 2 g

B (main color beads, shown in blue), 3 g

C (connector beads, shown in dark gray), 1 g

Nymo D or FireLine 6 lb

Size 10 beading needle

Microcrystalline wax

Scissors

Lighter

DIMENSIONS

2 inches (5 cm) wide

FIVE-POINTED STAR

When you modify the basic triangle by starting with a ring of four beads instead of three and increase four times in each row instead of three times, an interesting shape results. After the fourth row, the piece, which starts off as a square, begins to fold along the line of increases. When joined, the folded triangular shapes form the points of a three-dimensional star.

If you want to further experiment with this design, you can make each unit as large as you wish. A five-unit, five-pointed star will have a slightly domed center. Larger units flatten out the center dome.

First Unit

With 2 yards (about 2 m) of thread in your needle, bring the ends together, wax well, knot, clip the tail close to the knot, and melt the ends slightly.

Note: When making a star with more than five units (points), work with medium to soft tension.

Row 1: String 4 As and form a ring secured with a lark's head knot as follows: Push the beads to within 1 inch (2.5 cm) of the knot. Separate the strands between the beads and the knot. Pass the needle between the strands, tighten, then pass back through the last bead strung (**figures 1** and **2**). Don't allow the knot to slip into a bead. Orient the work so you're working counterclockwise (lefties, work clockwise).

figure 1

figure 2

Row 2: *Add 2 As and pass through the next A. Repeat from * three more times. Step up (**figure 3**).

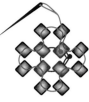

figure 3

Note: These beads form the corners of the unit.

Row 3: *Add 2 As and pass through the next A. Peyote once with B. Repeat from * three more times. Step up (**figure 4**).

figure 4

Row 4: *Add 2 As and pass through the next A. Peyote twice with B. Repeat from * three more times. Step up (**figure 5**).

figure 5

Rows 5–10: Work as for row 4. Increase the number of peyote stitches on each side by one with each new row. Continue to add 2 As at each corner.

Your unit will look like **figure 6** when you fold it.

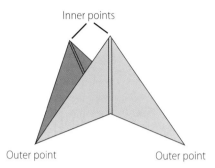

Inner points

Outer point   Outer point

figure 6

Row 11: Use C to add connector beads to each of the four sides of this unit, adding 1 C at each corner. End with the thread exiting a single C at a corner. Weave in the thread and clip.

Second, Third, and Fourth Units

Make the next three units as for rows 1–10 of the first unit. Add 1 C at the current corner, then join to the previous unit as described on the next page.

Connect the Units

Fold the second unit so the thread is at an inner point (**figure 7**). Align the second unit with the first unit and zip them together along one side. At the outer point, after exiting the first A (of the pair) in the second unit, pass through the single C at the tip of the first unit, then pass through the second A in the second unit and a single C at the fourth corner. Continue zipping the second side of the two units.

After zipping two sides together, add a single bead on the inner point of the second unit, then add connector (C) beads to the remaining two sides of the second unit. Weave in the tail and clip.

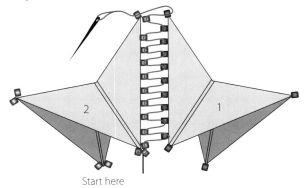

Note that the single bead at the outer point on the first unit will fit between the pair of beads on the point of the second unit.

figure 7

Fifth Unit

Make and connect one more unit, but don't add connector beads to the fifth unit. When adding the last unit, connector beads will already be in place for the sides but not the points, so you'll need to add them as you zip. Weave in the tail and clip.

Note: When making a star with several units, fold the units like an accordion.

Variation with Radiating Stripes

Work two rows with A and two rows with B. Make the last row of the unit the same as the beginning color, then use that same color for the connector beads.

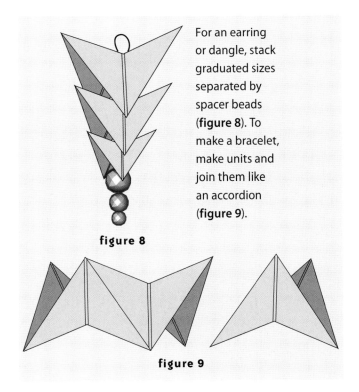

For an earring or dangle, stack graduated sizes separated by spacer beads (**figure 8**). To make a bracelet, make units and join them like an accordion (**figure 9**).

figure 8

figure 9

BLUE NOVA STAR PENDANT

This nine-pointed star makes a bold statement when worn on a gold chain.

First Unit

With 2 yards (about 2 m) of thread in your needle, bring the ends together, wax well, knot, clip the tail close to the knot, and melt the ends slightly. Orient the work so you are working counterclockwise (lefties, work clockwise). Work with medium tension.

Note: Use A for the connector beads.

Rows 1–14: Make the first unit following the directions for the Five-Pointed Star on page 39, but work 14 rows instead of 10.

Row 15: Use A to add connector beads to each of the four sides of this unit, adding 1 A at each corner. End with the thread exiting a single A at a corner. Weave in the thread and clip.

Eight More Units

Make another eight units following the directions for rows 1–14 of the first unit. Join each unit to the previous one as for the Five-Pointed Star on page 39. Don't add connector beads to the ninth unit and don't zip the first unit to the ninth unit yet.

Core

Start a new doubled thread. String 18 As and form a ring secured with a lark's head knot as follows: Push the beads to within 1 inch (2.5 cm) of the knot. Separate the strands between the beads and the knot. Pass the needle between the strands, tighten, then pass back through the last bead strung. Work in even-count tubular peyote stitch until the core is ¾ inch (2 cm) long. (Even-count tubular peyote stitch has a step up at the end of each row.) Don't clip the thread.

Insert the core through the center of the partially connected units so the last stitched row of the core aligns with the inner points of the joined units. Zip the core's "up" beads to the single beads on the inner points of the joined units.

Weave through beads to the other end of the core. Zip the "up" beads to the point beads on this side of the star.

Note: Make sure the core isn't twisted inside the star. Once the core is in place, finish zipping the first and last units together. Weave in the thread and clip.

If your star needs to be firmer, dip it in liquid acrylic floor polish, shape it as you wish, then allow it to dry on waxed paper, turning it occasionally for the first few minutes to prevent the floor polish from draining out of the beads. Alternatively, use a paintbrush or cotton swab to apply acrylic floor polish to the outside of the star.

String the Pendant

Cut the chain into two 25-inch (63.5 cm) segments. Pass the end of one chain segment through the star's core. Align the ends of the chain and connect the two end links using a jump ring. Repeat with the remaining chain segment.

Attach the split ring to one jump ring and the clasp to the other jump ring.

SUPPLIES

Size 11° cylinder beads:

    A (shown in gold), 8 g

    B (shown in blue), 20 g

50 inches (127 cm) of chain

2 gold 4-mm jump rings

1 gold 6-mm split ring

1 lobster-claw clasp

Nymo D or FireLine 6 lb

Size 10 beading needle

Microcrystalline wax

Scissors

Lighter

2 pairs of round- or chain-nose pliers

Wire cutters

DIMENSIONS

3 inches (7.5 cm) in diameter

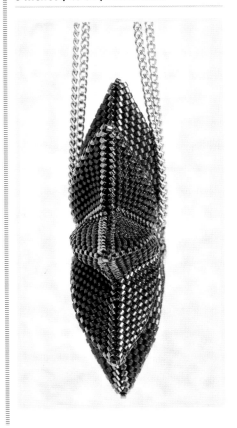

PARTY TIME NECKLACE

Make this necklace to wear with your best little black dress and have a sparkling time at your next party.

Folded Units—Make 12

With 2 yards (about 2 m) of thread in your needle, bring the ends together, wax well, knot, clip the tail close to the knot, and melt the ends slightly. Orient the work so you're working counter-clockwise (lefties, work clockwise).

Rows 1–10: Follow the directions for one unit of the Five-Pointed Star on page 39 through row 10, using one color of cylinder beads for this project instead of two.

Row 11: *After exiting the pair of beads at the corner, add 2 As, then pass back through the second bead, then through the second bead of the pair at this corner* (**figure 1**). Peyote around the next two sides of the unit. Repeat from * to *. Fold the unit and zip the edges together.

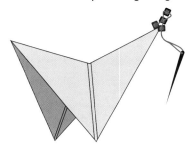

figure 1

Embellishment

Working with one unit at a time and stitching in the ditch, attach ten 2.5-mm crystals to each zipped edge and one 2.5-mm crystal to the center point (21 crystals on each unit). Use a B at the tip of each fringe. Sew a margarita to each unit's center front and center back.

Assemble the Necklace

String a 4-mm crystal onto the beading wire. String one corner point of one unit, seven 4-mm crystals, and the second corner point of that unit. Repeat with the remaining units and 4-mm crystals. End with one 4-mm crystal. Attach the clasp using crimp beads.

SUPPLIES

Size 11° cylinder beads:

   A (shown in black), 24 g

Size 15° seed beads:

   B (shown in crystal), 3 g

252 crystal AB 2.5-mm bicone crystals (Swarovski 5328)

24 crystal AB 5-mm margaritas (Swarovski 3700)

97 crystal AB 4-mm bicone crystals (Swarovski 5328)

18 inches (45.5 cm) of beading wire

2 crimp beads

Clasp

FireLine 6 lb

Size 10 beading needle

Microcrystalline wax

Scissors

Lighter

Crimping tool

Wire cutters

DIMENSIONS

16 inches (40.5 cm)

Chapter 3
TEARDROPS

This section begins with the basic elongated teardrop, which is used for the Radiance Pendant as well as for flower petals and leaves. A modified teardrop can create heart and butterfly shapes.

SUPPLIES

Size 11° cylinder beads, 3 g

Nymo D or FireLine 6 lb

Size 10 beading needle

Microcrystalline wax

Scissors

Lighter

BASIC ELONGATED TEARDROP

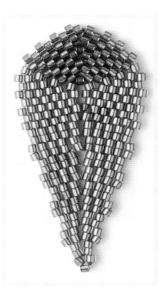

This teardrop shape is made using two peyote increase patterns: the triangle and the hexagon. To elongate the shape, work in two-drop peyote stitch on the pointed end. When working the two-drop section, always think of the two beads you're adding as a single bead.

With 2 yards (about 2 m) of thread in your needle, bring the ends together, wax well, knot, clip the tail close to the knot, and melt the ends slightly.

Note: In the diagrams below, new beads are outlined for clarity.

Row 1: String 11 beads and form a ring secured with a lark's head knot as follows: Push the beads to within 1 inch (2.5 cm) of the knot. Separate the strands between the beads and the knot. Pass the needle between the strands, tighten, then pass back through the last bead strung (**figure 1**). Don't allow the knot to slip into a bead. Orient the work so you're working counter-clockwise (lefties, work clockwise).

figure 1

Row 2: Add 4 beads and pass through the next bead. (Don't skip a bead here.)
• Peyote twice.
• *Add 1 bead and pass through the next bead. Repeat from * one time.
• Peyote once.

• Add 1 bead and pass through the next 3 beads (**figure 2**).

figure 2

Row 3: Add 4 beads and pass through the next 2 beads.
• Peyote twice.
• *Add 2 beads and pass through the next bead. Repeat from * two more times.
• Peyote once.
• Add 1 bead, skip 1 bead in the row below, and pass through the next 4 beads (**figure 3**).

figure 3

Row 4: Add 4 beads and pass through the next 2 beads.
• Add 2 beads and pass through the next bead.
• Peyote twice.
• *Add 1 bead between the next pair of beads and peyote once. Repeat from * two more times.
• Peyote once.
• Add 2 beads and pass through the next 4 beads (**figure 4**).

figure 4

Row 5: Add 4 beads and pass through the next 2 beads.
• Add 2 beads and pass through the next 2 beads.
• Peyote 10, passing through 2 beads after adding the 10th bead.
• Add 2 beads and pass through the next 4 beads (**figure 5**).

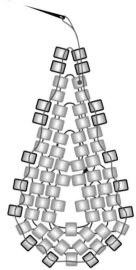

figure 5

Row 6: Add 4 beads and pass through the next 2 beads.
• Add 2 beads and pass through the next 2 beads.
• Add 2 beads and pass through 1 bead.
• Peyote twice.
• *Add 2 beads and pass through the next bead. Peyote once. Repeat from * two more times.
• Peyote once.
• Add 2 beads and pass through the next 2 beads.
• Add 2 beads and pass through the next 4 beads (**figure 6**).

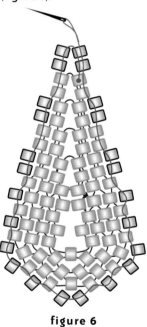

figure 6

Row 7: Add 4 beads and pass through the next 2 beads.
• Add 2 beads and pass through the next 2 beads twice.
• Peyote 3.
• *Add 1 bead between the next pair of beads. Peyote twice. Repeat from * two more times.
• Peyote once and pass through the next 2 beads.
• Add 2 beads and pass through the next 2 beads.
• Add 2 beads and pass through the next 4 beads (**figure 7**).

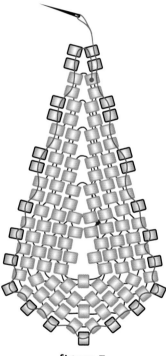

figure 7

Row 8: Add 4 beads and pass through the next 2 beads.
• Add 2 beads and pass through the next 2 beads twice.
• Add 2 beads and pass through 1 bead.
• Peyote 12.
• Add 2 beads and pass through 2 beads. Repeat one time.
• Add 2 beads and pass through the next 4 beads.

Row 9: Add 4 beads and pass through the next 2 beads.
• Add 2 beads and pass through the next 2 beads; repeat two more times.
• Peyote 3.
• *Add 2 beads and pass through the next "up" bead. Peyote twice. Repeat from * two more times.
• Peyote once.
• Add 2 beads and pass through the next 2 beads. Repeat one time.
• Add 2 beads and pass through the next 4 beads.

Row 10: Add 3 beads and pass through the next 2 beads.
• Add 2 beads and pass through the next 2 beads three times.
• Add 2 beads and pass through the next bead.
• Peyote 3.
• *Add 1 bead and pass through the next bead. Peyote 3. Repeat from * two more times.
• Add 2 beads and pass through 2 beads three times.
• Add 2 beads and pass through the next 3 beads.
• Weave in the thread and clip.

SUPPLIES

Size 11° cylinder beads, 3 g

Pin back, 1 inch (2.5 cm) long

Nymo D or FireLine 6 lb

Size 10 beading needle

Microcrystalline wax

Scissors

Lighter

DIMENSIONS

1½ x 1½ inches (4 x 4 cm)

HEART PIN

This symbol of love can be worn as a brooch, incorporated into other beadwork, or used as an embellishment on a very special Valentine's Day card.

1 Make two Basic Elongated Teardrops following the instructions on page 47. On the second teardrop, don't clip the thread.

2 With the thread exiting the bead around the corner from a tip bead at the end of row 10, add 2 beads and pass through the next 2 beads. Repeat three more times. Add 1 bead and pass through the next bead. Repeat two more times (**figure 1**).

3 To connect the teardrops, pass down through the bead opposite in the first teardrop. Zip the two edges together (**figure 2**). Weave in the thread and clip. Sew a pin back to one side.

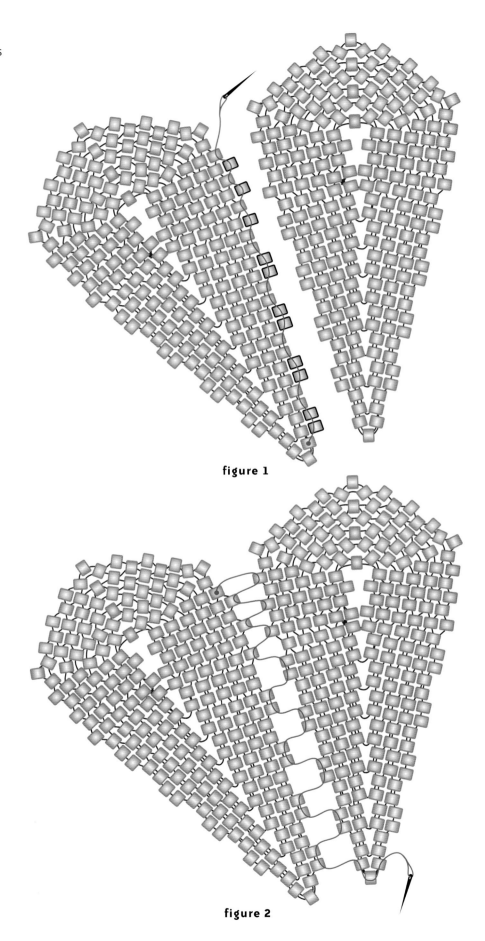

figure 1

figure 2

SUPPLIES

Size 11° cylinder beads:

A (shown in blue), 7 g

B (a darker shade of A, shown in dark blue), 2 g

C (diamond, shown in brown) 3 g

5 white 2.8-mm drops

1 crystal 5-mm rose montee

Nymo D or FireLine 6 lb

Size 10 beading needle

Microcrystalline wax

Scissors

Lighter

DIMENSIONS

3¼ x 3 inches (8.5 x 7.5 cm)

RADIANCE PENDANT

Joining five teardrop shapes creates a fan that suggests the radiating lines of the Art Deco style. A folded diamond shape embellished with tiny pearl drops and a rose montee serve as the bail. Wear the version shown here on a neck ring, cord, or chain; the variation on page 54 has a pin back with bail and can be worn as either a pin or a pendant.

With 2 yards (about 2 m) of thread in your needle, bring the ends together, wax well, knot, clip the tail close to the knot, and melt the ends slightly.

Make the Fan

To make the fan shape, follow the instructions for the Heart Pin on page 49, but use B beads instead of A for rows 9 and 10. Stitch and join three more teardrops. As you complete the third through fifth teardrops, continue with the existing thread to join each teardrop to the previous one (**figure 1**).

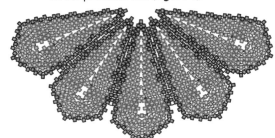

figure 1

Add the Diamond-Shaped Bail

For the bail, prepare the thread as for the teardrop. Work with soft tension so the diamond can be folded.

Note: In these instructions the corners are referred to as north, south, east, and west, as shown in **figure 2**.

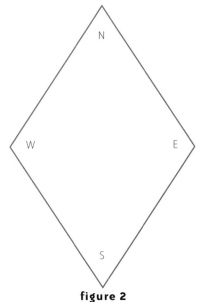

figure 2

Row 1: String 4 Cs and form a ring secured with a lark's head knot as follows: Push the beads to within 1 inch (2.5 cm) of the knot. Separate the strands between the beads and the knot. Pass the needle between the strands, tighten, then pass back through the last bead strung (**figure 3**). Don't let the knot slip inside a bead. Orient the work so you're working counterclockwise (lefties, work clockwise).

figure 3

Row 2: *Add 2 Cs and pass through the next C. Repeat from * three more times. Step up (**figure 4**).

figure 4

Note: The step up will always occur at the north corner.

Row 3: *Add 2 Cs and pass through the next C at the north corner. Don't skip a bead. Peyote once with C. Add 1 C between the pair at the corner. Peyote once with C. Repeat from * once. Step up (**figure 5**).

figure 5

Row 4: Add 2 Cs and pass through the next C at the north corner. Peyote 4 with C, passing through the single C at the west corner. Add 2 Cs and pass through the next C at the south corner. Peyote 4 with C, passing through the C at the east corner. Step up (**figure 6**).

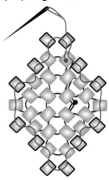

figure 6

Row 5: *Add 2 Cs and pass through the next C. Peyote twice with C. At the next corner, add 2 Cs (above the C added in row 3) and pass through the next C. Peyote twice with C. Repeat from * once. Step up (**figure 7**).

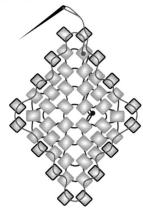

figure 7

Row 6: *Add 2 Cs and pass through the next C. Peyote 3 with C. At the next corner, add 1 C between the pair at the corner. Peyote 3 with C. Repeat from * once. Step up (**figure 8**).

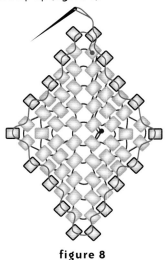

figure 8

Rows 7–12: Repeat rows 4–6 two more times. You'll have a total of 12 rows with eight beads sticking up on each side of the diamond, not counting the corner beads.

Note: Count rows easily by counting the pairs of beads from the center to the north end.

Row 13: Add 1 C at the corner and pass through the next bead without skipping a bead. Peyote 12 with C, passing through the single bead at the west corner. *Add 1 drop and pass through the next 3 beads (an "up" bead, a "down" bead, and an "up" bead). Repeat from * once. Add 1 drop between the pair of

beads at the bottom point. Stitch the right side of the diamond as a mirror image of the left side (**figure 9**).

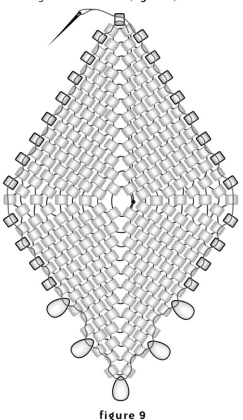

figure 9

Assembly

Fold the diamond in half, north over south. Place the top edge of the fan shape inside the folded diamond, leaving a channel between the folded edge of the diamond and the top of the fan for the cord or neck ring.

Sew the diamond in place over the fan as follows: Exiting a side corner bead of the front diamond and holding the fan in place, poke through the fan to the back, pass through a bead in the diamond, then poke back to the front. Continue around the folded diamond.

Stitch the rose montee in place on the front of the diamond. Weave in the thread and clip.

Radiance Earrings

Stitch two fans consisting of four elongated teardrops worked through row 7 of the Basic Elongated Teardrop on page 47. Work two diamonds through row 9. Sew one diamond over each fan and embellish with a rose montee. Sew small jump rings or wire guards to the top of each diamond and attach earring findings to the jump rings.

Radiance Pin with Button

Work and join five teardrop shapes. Center a ½–⅝-inch (12–14-mm) button along the flat edge and sew it into place. Stitch a pin back to the back.

SUPPLIES

Size 11° cylinder beads:

A (shown in rust), 7 g

B (a darker shade of A, shown in dark rust), 2 g

C (diamond, shown in dark gray), 5 g

9 white 2.8-mm drop beads

1 white 4-mm pearl

1 black 6-mm rondelle

1 black 15 x 9-mm faceted drop with vertical hole

1 flat-back 12-mm stone (Swarovski 2006 or 2072, or sew-on stone Swarovski 3200, 3204, or 3700)

1 pin back with bail, 1¼ inches (3.2 cm) long

Clear glue (E6000 or 527 Bond)

Nymo D or FireLine 6 lb

Size 10 beading needle

Microcrystalline wax

Scissors

Lighter

Cotton swab

Rubbing alcohol

DIMENSIONS

3¼ x 3¼ inches (8.5 x 8.5 cm)

This version features a fan with a two-layered diamond accented with a drop at the bottom and a cabochon that's glued in place. Wear this as either a pin or a pendant by sewing a pin back with a bail to the back.

Make the Fan

Follow the directions for the Radiance Pendant on page 52 to make and join five teardrop shapes into a fan.

First Diamond Layer

Rows 1–6: Follow the instructions for the diamond-shaped bail on page 52, working rows 1–6.

Rows 7–14: Repeat rows 4–6 twice. Then work rows 4 and 5 one more time.

Row 15: Work as for row 6, but add only one bead at the north and south corners. You'll have nine "up" beads on each side, not counting the corner beads (**figure 1**).

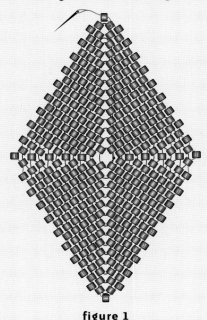

figure 1

Second Diamond Layer

Make the second diamond like the first, but work only through row 14. You'll have two beads at each of the four corners. Don't clip the thread.

Join the Diamonds

Using the thread from the second diamond, pass through beads to the first of the two beads at the west corner. Lay the second diamond on top of the first diamond and pass through the single bead at the west corner of the first diamond. Continue to zip the outer edges together on the lower half only.

Attach the Fan

Place the fan between the open end of the two diamond layers and sew it in place as follows: Exit a single side corner bead on the front diamond and,

holding the fan in place, poke between the beads through to the back, pass through a bead in the diamond, then poke back to the front. Continue around the upper half of the diamond.

Add Drop Beads

Add the 9 drop beads to the upper half of the diamond as follows: Exiting a single corner bead of row 15 of the front diamond, pass through the next three beads (an "up" bead, a "down" bead, and an "up" bead). Add 1 drop bead and pass through the second bead along the edge. Continue to add drops as shown in **figure 2**.

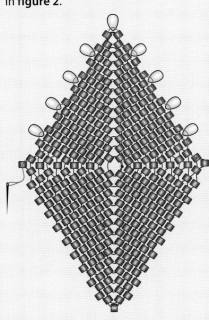

figure 2

Attach the Dangle

With the thread anchored in the bottom of the diamond, exit the single cylinder bead at the south corner. Add the pearl, rondelle, faceted drop, and 1 cylinder bead. Pass back through the drop, rondelle, and pearl and enter the bottom cylinder bead from the opposite side. Repeat to reinforce, then weave in the

thread, knot it, weave through a few more beads, and clip (**figure 3**).

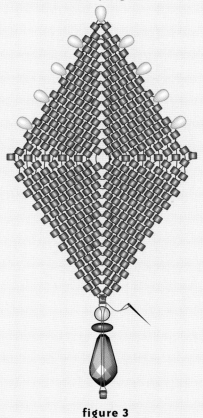

figure 3

Sew On the Pin Back with Bail

Center the pin back with bail on the fan so the top of the bail is about ¼ inch (6 mm) from the top. Sew the pin back in place.

Glue the Cabochon

Dip a cotton swab into rubbing alcohol and squeeze out the excess liquid. Wipe the center of the diamond with the swab and allow it to dry. Glue the cabochon to the center of the diamond with E6000 or 527 Bond glue. Let dry.

Wear the piece as a pin or a pendant with a chain or neck ring. To add a neck ring, it might be necessary to open the bail slightly with pliers and close it after inserting the neck ring.

TINY BUTTERFLIES

**Whether you use them for pins, hair clips, or embellishments in
other beadwork, these tiny butterflies add a touch of lightness
and whimsy to any project. They're made with two large and two
small teardrop shapes.**

Overview

The upper wings have six rows each; the
lower wings, five rows. Join the upper
wings to the lower wings in the middle
of row 5.

Upper Wings

With 2 yards (about 2 m) of thread in
your needle, bring the ends together,
wax well, knot, clip the tail close to the
knot, and melt the ends slightly.

Row 1: String 11 As and form a ring
secured with a lark's head knot as follows: Push the beads to within 1 inch

(2.5 cm) of the knot. Separate the
strands between the beads and the
knot. Pass the needle between the
strands, tighten, then pass back through
the last bead strung (**figure 1**). Don't
allow the knot to slip into a bead. Orient
the work so you're working counterclockwise (lefties, work clockwise).

figure 1

Row 2: Add 2 As and pass through the next A.
• Peyote twice with A.
• *Add 1 A and pass through the next A without skipping a bead. Repeat from * one time.
• Peyote twice with A. Step up after the second stitch (**figure 2**).

figure 2

Row 3: Add 2 As and pass through the next A.
• Peyote twice with A.
• *Add 2 As and pass through the next A. Repeat from * two more times.
• Peyote twice with A. Step up after the second stitch (**figure 3**).

figure 3

Row 4: Add 2 As and pass through the next A.
• Peyote 3 with A.
• *Add 1 A, pass through the next A, then peyote once with A. Repeat from * two more times.
• Peyote twice with A. Step up after the second stitch (**figure 4**).

figure 4

Row 5: Add 2 As and pass through the next A.
• Peyote 12 with A. Step up after the last stitch (**figure 5**).

figure 5

Row 6: Add 2 As and pass through the next A.
• Peyote 4 with A.
• *Add 2 As, pass through the next A, then peyote once with A. Repeat from * two more times.
• Peyote 3 with A. Step up after the last stitch (**figure 6**).

figure 6

Row 7: Add 2 As and pass through the next A.
• Peyote 5 with A.
• *Add 1 A, pass through the next A, then peyote twice with A. Repeat from * two more times.
• Peyote 3 with A. Step up after the last stitch (**figure 7**).

figure 7

Make a second upper wing.

Lower Wings

Make two lower wings following the directions for the upper wings through row 6, using B beads instead of A (**figure 8**). Don't clip the thread.

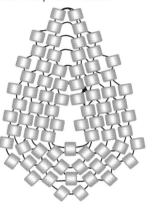
figure 8

Join the Lower and Upper Wings

With the thread exiting the B on the lower wing's top right, add 1 B and pass through the next B without skipping a bead. Zip the lower wing to the upper wing beginning with the third bead along the edge of the upper wing (the second "up" bead). Continue to zip until the thread is exiting the fourth "up" bead in the upper wing (**figure 9**). Knot, weave in the thread, and clip. Repeat to join the remaining upper and lower wings.

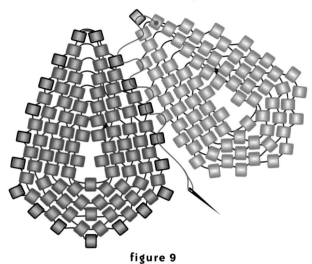

figure 9

Join the Two Pairs of Wings

Join the two end beads on the upper wings, and then the two single beads at the end of each lower wing as shown in **figure 10** and the detail in **figure 11**.

Stitch a bugle bead or pointed sew-on to the front for the body.

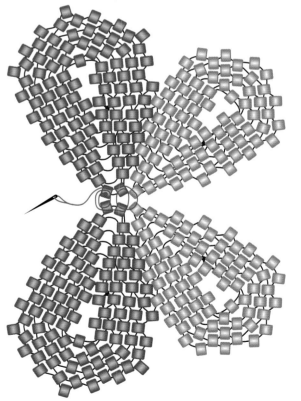

figure 10

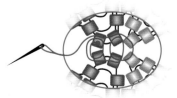

figure 11

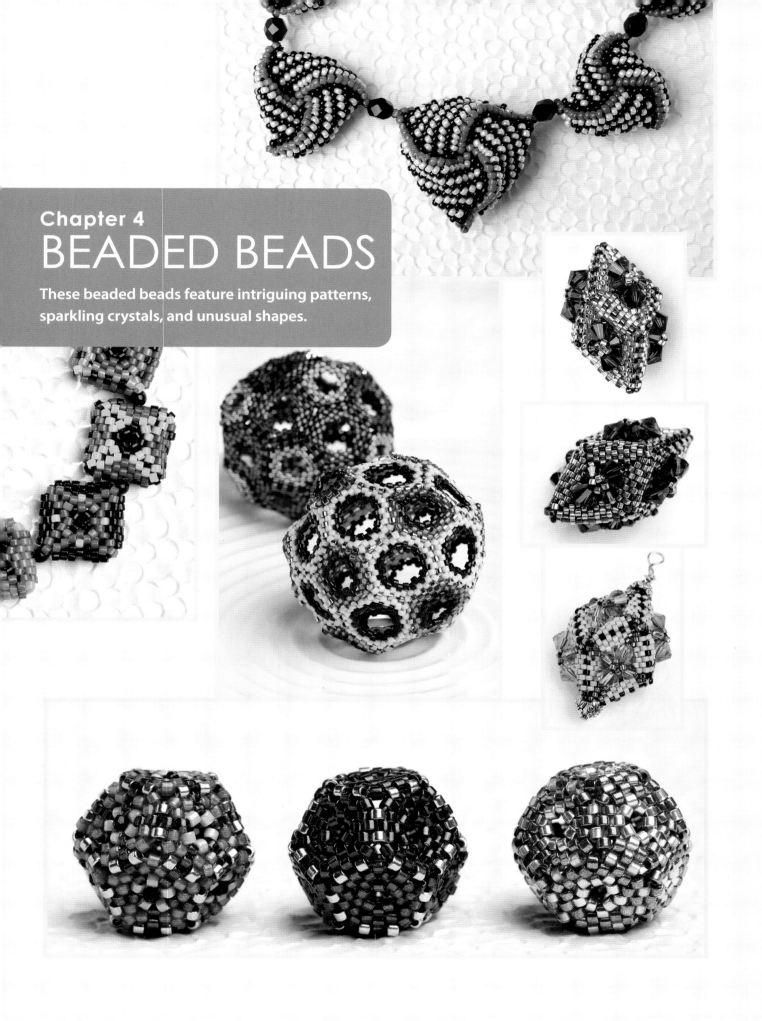

Chapter 4
BEADED BEADS

These beaded beads feature intriguing patterns,
sparkling crystals, and unusual shapes.

SUPPLIES

Size 11° cylinder beads:

A (shown in yellow), < 1 g

B (shown in red), < 1 g

Nymo D or FireLine 6 lb

Size 10 beading needle

Microcrystalline wax

Scissors

Lighter

Wire cutters (optional)

DIMENSIONS

⅝ inch (1.5 cm) square

PILLOW BEAD

Bet you can't make just one of these! You'll see patterns emerge like a kaleidoscope on these square, two-layered beads if you work with three or four silver-lined or opaque colors. String them corner to corner, edge to edge, or front to back.

Basic Square—First Layer

With 1 yard (about 1 m) of thread in your needle, bring the ends together, wax well, knot, clip the tail close to the knot, and melt the ends slightly.

Row 1: String 4 As and form a ring secured with a lark's head knot as follows: Push the beads to within 1 inch (2.5 cm) of the knot. Separate the strands between the beads and the knot. Pass the needle between the strands, tighten, then pass back through the last bead strung (**figure 1**). Don't

allow the knot to slip inside a bead. Orient the work so you're working counterclockwise (lefties, work clockwise).

Row 2: *Add 1 B and pass through the next A. Repeat from * three more times. Step up (**figure 2**).

figure 2

figure 1

Row 3: *Add 3 As and pass through the next B. Repeat from * three more times. Step up (**figure 3**). Push down the middle bead of the three, as shown in this figure. These beads form the corners of the square.

figure 3

Row 4: *Add 2 As and pass through the third A of the set of three beads at the corner. Add 1 B, skip 1 B in the row below, and pass through the next A. Repeat from * three more times. Step up (**figure 4**).

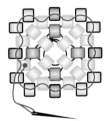

figure 4

Row 5: *Add 2 As and pass through the next A at this corner. Peyote twice with B. Repeat from * three more times. Step up (**figure 5**).

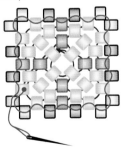

figure 5

Row 6: *Add 1 A and pass through the next A at this corner. Peyote 3 with B. Repeat from * three more times. Step up (**figure 6**).

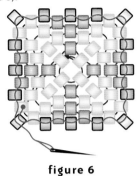

figure 6

Row 7: *Peyote 4 with B. Repeat from * three more times. Step up (**figure 7**).

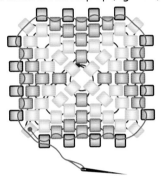

figure 7

Row 8: *Peyote 3 with B and once with A. Repeat from * three more times. Step up (**figure 8**). Pull tight so the last two rows form the sides of the pillow bead. Weave in the thread and clip.

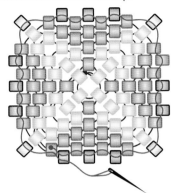

figure 8

Basic Square—Second Layer

Work rows 1–7 to make the second layer. Zip the second layer to the first, aligning the corner beads. Weave in the thread and clip.

Variation

To create holes in the pillow beads for stringing, break beads in opposite corners or at the center of opposite sides of row 8 of the first layer. Use wire cutters and be careful not to clip the threads. For information on how to string beaded beads, see page 14.

CORNERLESS CUBE BEAD

Shaped like a simple cube with the corners cut off, this beaded bead consists of six squares and eight triangles.

If you don't have experience making triangles or squares, stitch your first Cornerless Cube Bead using only two colors. Then try the more complex versions. Seven of my patterns for four-color beads start on page 66, plus there's a blank grid for you to design your own.

When selecting colors, choose beads in opaque, metallic, or matte finishes with good contrast. These colors will ensure that the patterns created in the tiny space of the bead surface will be distinguishable and that colors will not blur or merge with adjoining colors.

Squares

Make six squares following the directions for rows 1–6 of the Pillow Bead's basic square on page 61. On the last row, you'll have a single bead at each corner and three "up" beads between corner beads. After completing each square, weave in the thread and clip.

Triangles

With 2 yards (about 2 m) of thread in your needle, bring the ends together, wax well, knot, clip the tail close to the knot, and melt the ends slightly.

Row 1: String 3 As and form a ring secured with a lark's head knot as follows: Push the beads to within 1 inch (2.5 cm) of the knot. Separate the strands between the beads and the knot. Pass the needle between the strands, tighten, then pass back through the last bead strung (**figures 1** and **2**). Don't allow the knot to slip inside a bead. Orient the work so you're working counterclockwise (lefties, work clockwise).

figure 1

figure 2

Row 2: *Add 2 As and pass through the next A. Repeat from * two more times. Step up (**figure 3**).

figure 3

Note: These beads form the three corners of the triangle. Make sure the pairs of beads at each corner sit almost parallel to each other. Adjust them if necessary.

Row 3: *Add 2 As and pass through the next A. Add 1 B, skip one bead in the row below, and pass through the next A. Repeat from * two more times. Step up (**figure 4**).

figure 4

Row 4: *Add 3 As and pass through the next A. Peyote twice with B. Repeat from * two more times. Step up (**figure 5**).

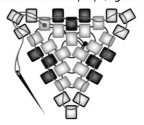

figure 5

Join Triangles to the First Square

Continuing with the thread from the triangle, zip the triangle to the side of a square (**figure 6**). Weave in the thread and clip.

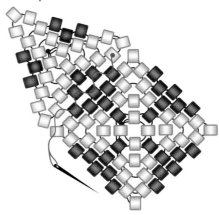

figure 6

Make and join three more triangles to the sides of the first square (**figure 7**). After joining the fourth triangle, don't clip the thread.

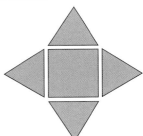

figure 7

Join the Second Through Fifth Squares

Pass the thread of the fourth triangle to its outer tip so the thread exits the A next to the corner. Zip one side of another square to the side of the triangle.

At the corner where the two triangles and two squares meet, pass through the four corner beads in a circular fashion as shown, then zip the next side of the square to the next triangle (**figure 8**).

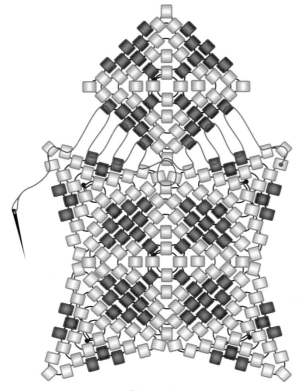

figure 8

Repeat this step, adding three more squares (**figure 9**). Weave in the thread and clip.

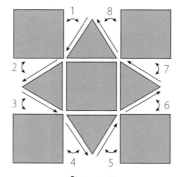

figure 9

Complete the Bead

Make another triangle, then zip the triangle between two squares. Weave in the thread and clip after adding each triangle. Repeat three times. Zip the sixth square to the four triangles to close the cube (**figure 10**). Weave in the thread and clip.

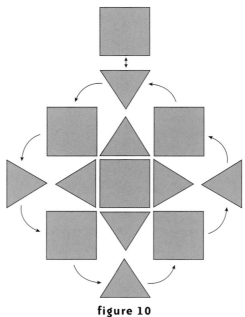

figure 10

Making Cornerless Cube Beads in Different Sizes

To make a smaller bead: On the triangles, skip row 3; on the squares, skip row 5.

For a larger bead: On the triangles, repeat row 3 once; on the squares, repeat row 5 once.

SUPPLIES FOR ONE BEAD

Size 11° cylinder beads:

Light, 1.5 g

Medium, 1.5 g

Dark, 1.5 g

Metallic, 1.5 g

Nymo D or FireLine 6 lb

Size 10 beading needle

Microcrystalline wax

Scissors

Lighter

DIMENSIONS

1⅛ inches (2.9 cm) in diameter

MOORISH TILE BEADS

Create an endless variety of patterns by varying the color arrangements in the triangles and squares that make up a Cornerless Cube Bead. When you join the shapes, new designs emerge from the connections.

Enjoy these patterns for the seven beads in this necklace. I'm sure you'll want to try designing Cornerless Cube Beads of your own.

Note: Beads are numbered from left to right as in **figure 1**.

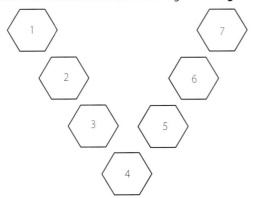

figure 1

Color Key

Light = L

Medium = M

Dark = D

Metallic = X

Bead 1

Triangle

Row	Corners	Sides
Row 1:	XXX	-
Row 2:	MM	-
Row 3:	DD	D
Row 4:	DXD	DD

Row 1

Row 2

Row 3

Row 4

Square

Row	Corners	Sides
Row 1:	XXXX	-
Row 2:	-	M
Row 3:	DMD	-
Row 4:	DD	L
Row 5:	DD	LL
Row 6:	X	DLD

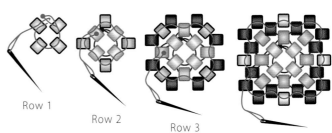
Row 1
Row 2
Row 3
Row 4

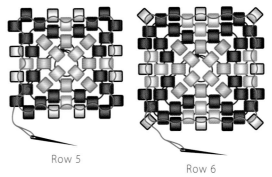
Row 5
Row 6

Bead 2

Triangle

Row	Corners	Sides
Row 1:	DDD	-
Row 2:	MM	-
Row 3:	LL	D
Row 4:	XXX	MM

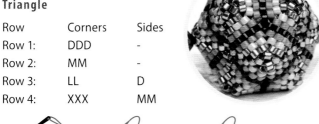

Row 1

Row 2

Row 3

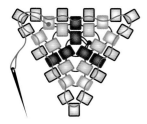

Row 4

Square

Row	Corners	Sides
Row 1:	XXXX	-
Row 2:	-	D
Row 3:	MXM	-
Row 4:	XX	D
Row 5:	XX	MM
Row 6:	X	LDL

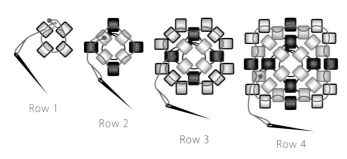

Row 1

Row 2

Row 3

Row 4

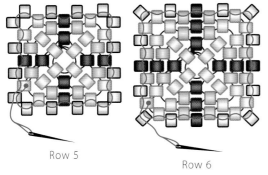

Row 5

Row 6

Bead 3

Triangle

Row	Corners	Sides
Row 1:	XXX	-
Row 2:	MM	-
Row 3:	DD	D
Row 4:	DDD	DD

Row 1

Row 2

Row 3

Row 4

Square

Row	Corners	Sides
Row 1:	XXXX	-
Row 2:	-	M
Row 3:	LML	-
Row 4:	LL	D
Row 5:	LL	DD
Row 6:	L	DDD

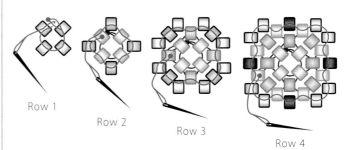

Row 1

Row 2

Row 3

Row 4

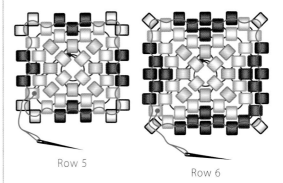

Row 5

Row 6

Bead 4

Triangle

Row	Corners	Sides
Row 1:	MMM	-
Row 2:	MM	-
Row 3:	MM	D
Row 4:	MMM	DD

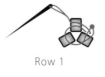

Row 1

Row 2

Row 3

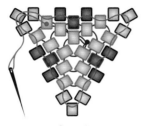

Row 4

Square

Row	Corners	Sides
Row 1:	LLLL	-
Row 2:	-	D
Row 3:	DMD	-
Row 4:	MM	X
Row 5:	MM	DD
Row 6:	M	DXD

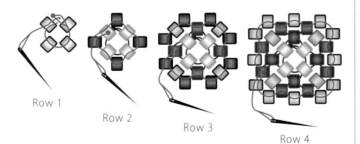

Row 1

Row 2

Row 3

Row 4

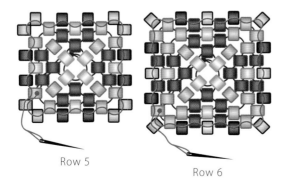

Row 5

Row 6

Bead 5

Triangle

Row	Corners	Sides
Row 1:	MMM	-
Row 2:	XX	-
Row 3:	DD	M
Row 4:	DLD	XX

Row 1

Row 2

Row 3

Row 4

Square

Row	Corners	Sides
Row 1:	DDDD	-
Row 2:	-	M
Row 3:	XDX	-
Row 4:	DD	M
Row 5:	DD	XX
Row 6:	L	DMD

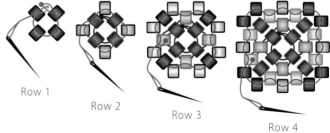

Row 1

Row 2

Row 3

Row 4

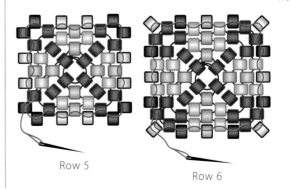

Row 5

Row 6

Bead 6

Triangle

Row	Corners	Sides
Row 1:	LLL	-
Row 2:	DD	-
Row 3:	XX	L
Row 4:	MMM	DD

Row 1

Row 2

Row 3

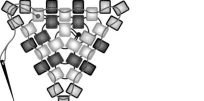

Row 4

Square

Row	Corners	Sides
Row 1:	MMMM	-
Row 2:	-	L
Row 3:	DXD	-
Row 4:	XX	L
Row 5:	XX	DD
Row 6:	M	XLX

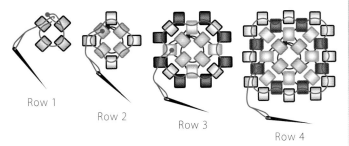

Row 1

Row 2

Row 3

Row 4

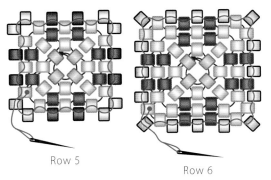

Row 5

Row 6

Bead 7

Triangle

Row	Corners	Sides
Row 1:	XXX	-
Row 2:	LL	-
Row 3:	DD	D
Row 4:	XXX	DD

Row 1

Row 2

Row 3

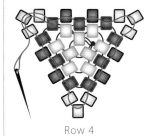

Row 4

Square

Row	Corners	Sides
Row 1:	DDDD	-
Row 2:	-	D
Row 3:	DLD	-
Row 4:	MM	X
Row 5:	XX	MM
Row 6:	X	DMD

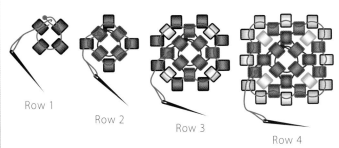

Row 1

Row 2

Row 3

Row 4

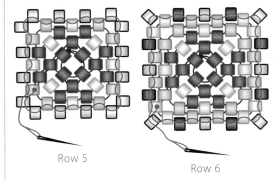

Row 5

Row 6

Variation

This *Moorish Tile Bead Necklace in Three Colors* contains four Cornerless Cube Beads and two smaller Cornerless Cube Beads, all worked in three colors.

Variation

Ancient Afghani jewelry, lost for centuries and recently rediscovered, inspired the components for this *Tillya Tepe Necklace*. It includes Cornerless Cube Beads in two colors and worked in peyote stitch, a wood bead covered with netting (see *Diane Fitzgerald's Favorite Projects* for instructions on making this), and a peyote-stitched Chandelier Bead (directions also appear in *Diane Fitzgerald's Shaped Beadwork*).

You may photocopy these blank grids to create and color your own patterns.

TINY DODECA BEAD

This hollow beaded bead is made up of 12 pentagons.
Vary the colors to create different patterns and designs.

SUPPLIES FOR EACH BEAD

Size 11° cylinder beads:

A (shown in blue), 2 g

B (shown in yellow), 1 g

Nymo D or FireLine 6 lb

Size 10 beading needle

Microcrystalline wax

Scissors

Lighter

DIMENSIONS

⅝ inch (1.5 cm) in diameter

First Pentagon

With 2 yards (about 2 m) of thread in your needle, bring the ends together, wax well, knot, clip the tail close to the knot, and melt the ends slightly.

Row 1: String 10 As and form a ring secured with a lark's head knot as follows: Push the beads to within 1 inch (2.5 cm) of the knot. Separate the strands between the beads and the knot. Pass the needle between the strands, tighten, then pass back through the last bead strung (**figure 1**). Don't allow the knot to slip inside a bead. Orient the work so you're working counter-clockwise (lefties, work clockwise).

figure 1

Row 2: *Add 2 As and pass through the second bead in the row below. Repeat from * four more times (**figure 2**).

figure 2

Row 3: *Add 1 A and pass through the second bead of the pair, then peyote once with A. Repeat from * four more times (**figure 3**).

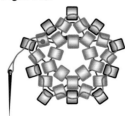

figure 3

Row 4: Peyote around with B. Weave in the thread and clip (**figure 4**).

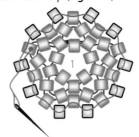

figure 4

Second Pentagon

Repeat rows 1–3. On row 4, zip the second pentagon to the first, then peyote around four sides with B (**figure 5**). Weave in the thread and clip.

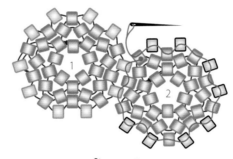

figure 5

Third Pentagon

Repeat rows 1–3. On row 4, zip the third pentagon to the first and second pentagons, then peyote around three sides with B (**figure 6**). Weave in the thread and clip.

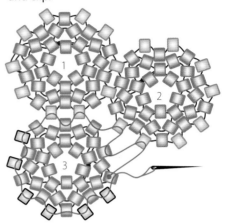

figure 6

Fourth and Fifth Pentagons

Repeat rows 1–3. On row 4, zip the new pentagon to the first pentagon and the previous one, then peyote around three sides with B (**figure 7**). Weave in the thread and clip.

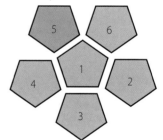

figure 7

Sixth Pentagon

Still referring to **figure 7**, repeat rows 1–3. On row 4, zip the sixth pentagon to the first, second, and fifth pentagons, then peyote around two sides with B. Weave in the thread and clip.

Make and join six more pentagons as described above, but don't add beads along the outer edge (row 4) of the second through sixth pentagons. The connector beads are already in place on the first half.

Zip the two halves together (**figures 8** and **9**). When joining the corners, pass through the three beads in a circular fashion, then continue with the next side.

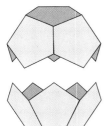

figure 8

figure 9

Weave in the thread. (Leave a short length of thread to hold on to if you plan to dip the bead in acrylic floor polish to stiffen it.)

Spike Balls

These beads are made with 12 pentagons, as described in the Soccer Ball Bead Variation with Crystals on page 89, but replace the crystals with 17 x 12-mm spike beads and assemble as described for the Tiny Dodeca Bead.

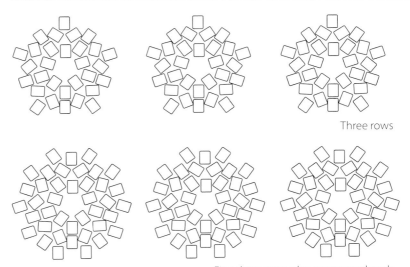

Three rows

First three rows plus connector beads

Photocopy these patterns to create your own designs.

SUPPLIES

Size 11° cylinder beads:

> **A (shown in pink), 7 g**

> **B (shown in gray), 4 g**

20 amethyst 6-mm bicone crystals (Swarovski 5328)

20 amethyst 4-mm bicone crystals (Swarovski 5328)

17 inches (43 cm) of chain

1 head pin, 1½ inches (4 cm) long

2 eye pins, 1½ inches (4 cm) long

2 jump rings or split rings

Clasp

FireLine 6 lb

Size 10 beading needle

Microcrystalline wax

Scissors

Lighter

Round-nose pliers

Wire cutters

DIMENSIONS

Necklace: 20½ inches (52 cm)

Pendant: 1½ inches (3.8 cm)

RHOMBO BEAD NECKLACE

A Rhombo Bead is actually a rhombohedron, a three-dimensional form made up of six diamond shapes (figure 1). My version has bicone crystals at the center of each diamond. You can also make two- or three-sided variations.

Make this necklace using one large, six-sided Rhombo Bead and two smaller ones. The smaller Rhombo Beads shown here are my flat, two-sided variation.

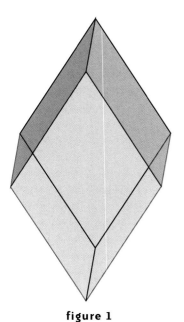

figure 1

Large Rhombo Bead: Upper Half—First Diamond

With 2 yards (about 2 m) of thread in your needle, bring the ends together, wax well, knot, clip the tail close to the knot, and melt the ends slightly.

Note: In these instructions the corners are referred to as north, south, east, and west, as shown in **figure 2**. The corners of each diamond are worked differently. For the north and south corners, you'll use a triangle increase and 6-mm bicones. For the east and west corners, you'll use a hexagon increase and 4-mm bicones.

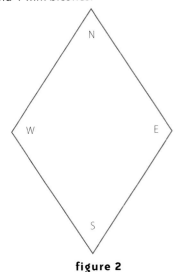

figure 2

Row 1: String 4 As (or use B beads if they provide better contrast) and form a ring secured with a lark's head knot as follows: Push the beads to within 1 inch (2.5 cm) of the knot. Separate the strands between the beads and the knot. Pass the needle between the strands, tighten, then pass back through the last bead strung (**figures 3** and **4**). Don't allow the knot to slip inside a bead. Orient the work so you're working counterclockwise (lefties, work clockwise).

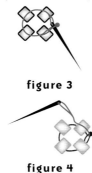

figure 3

figure 4

Row 2: *Add one 6-mm bicone and 2 As. Pass back through the bicone and the next bead on the beginning ring. Add one 4-mm bicone and 1 A. Pass back through the bicone and the next bead on the beginning ring. Repeat from * once. Step up through the 6-mm bicone and the first A (**figure 5**).

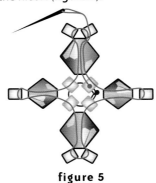

figure 5

Note: The step up always occurs at the north corner.

Row 3: *Add 2 As and pass through the next A at this corner. Add 5 As and pass through the single A at the next corner. Add 5 As and pass through the first A at the next corner. Repeat from * once.

Step up (**figure 6**). Pull tight, allowing the crystals to bulge forward a little.

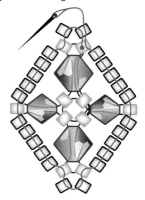

figure 6

Row 4: *Add 2 As and pass through the next A at this corner. Peyote 3 with A. Add 2 As above the single bead at the next corner. Peyote 3 with A. Repeat from * once. Step up (**figure 7**).

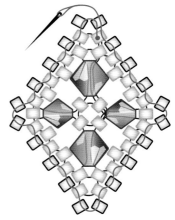

figure 7

Row 5: Add 2 As and pass through the next A at the north corner. Peyote 4 with A. Add 1 A between the pair of As at the west corner. Peyote 4 with A. Add 1 A and pass through the second bead of the pair of As at the south corner. Peyote 4 with A. Add 1 A between the pair of As at the east corner. Peyote 4 with A. Step up (**figure 8**).

Note: When you stitch row 5, notice that the north corner has 2 As and the south corner has only 1 A.

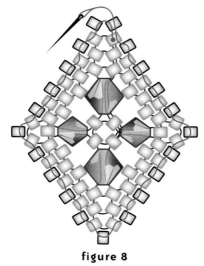

figure 8

Row 6: Add 1 A and pass through the next A at this corner. Peyote 20 with B, passing through the single A at the west, south, and east corners and ending at the north corner (**figure 9**). Weave in the thread and clip.

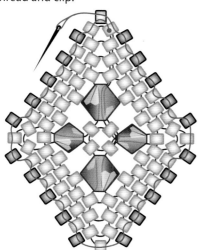

figure 9

Large Rhombo Bead: Upper Half—Second Diamond

Make the second diamond like the first, but work only rows 1–5.

Add 1 A and pass through the next A at the north corner. Zip the northwest side of the second diamond to the northeast side of the first diamond (**figure 10**). Peyote around the rest of the second diamond with B. Weave in the thread and clip.

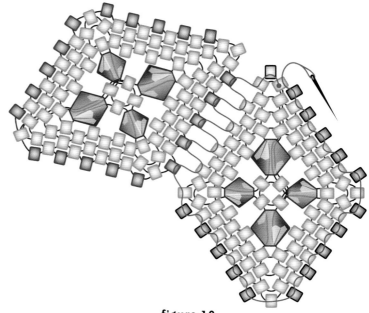

figure 10

Large Rhombo Bead: Upper Half—Third Diamond

Make the third diamond like the second and zip to the previous diamond as described above. Continue to add B beads around the lower half of the third diamond. After passing through the single corner bead at the east corner, zip the northeast side of the third diamond to the first diamond. At the top, where the three north corners meet, pass through the 3 Bs (**figure 11**). Weave in the thread and clip.

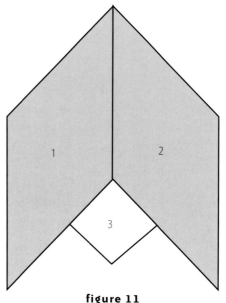

figure 11

Large Rhombo Bead: Lower Half

Note: The lower half assembly differs from the upper half because the upper half already has connector beads added.

Make three diamonds as above, working only rows 1–5. On the first two diamonds, end with row 5, weave in the thread, and clip. After completing the third diamond, leave the thread attached.

With the thread exiting the right A of the third diamond's north corner, add 1 A and pass through the next A at this corner. Peyote along the northwest side with B. After exiting the single A on the west corner, pass through the single A at the east corner of the second diamond, then pass back through the last B added on the previous diamond.

Continue zipping back to the north corner of the second diamond. Pass through the right A of the second diamond's north corner, add 1 A, and exit through the left A of the second diamond's north corner (**figure 12**).

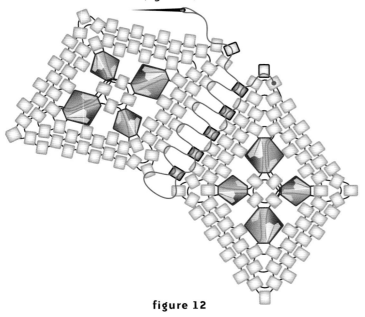

figure 12

Connect the third lower-half diamond between the first and second diamonds in the same way.

Note: As you connect the large diamonds, they must all be oriented with the north corners adjacent to each other. The north corners have four pairs of beads; the south corners, three pairs.

Join the Upper and Lower Halves

Pass the thread through beads so it exits a single corner bead at an east or a west corner. Align the upper and lower halves, inserting points into valleys, and zip the two halves together (**figure 13**). Where the corners meet, pass through all three As and pull tight. Then continue to zip the sides. Weave in the thread and clip.

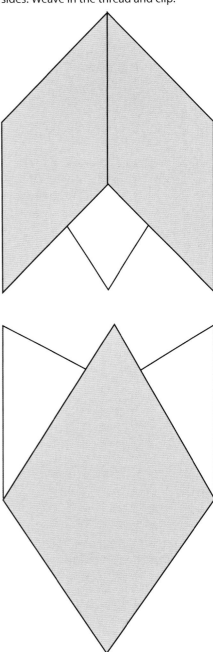

figure 13

Flat Rhombo Bead— First Diamond

With 2 yards (about 2 m) of thread in your needle, bring the ends together, wax well, knot, clip the tail close to the knot, and melt the ends slightly.

Rows 1–4: Follow the directions through row 4 for the Large Rhombo Bead's first upper-half diamond. Your thread will exit the north corner after row 4.

Row 5: *Add 2 As and pass through the next A at this corner. Peyote 4 with A. Add 1 A between the pair of As at the next corner. Peyote 4 with A. Repeat from * once. Step up (**figure 14**). Weave in the thread and clip on the first layer.

figure 14

Row 6: *Add 2 Bs and pass through the next A at this corner. Peyote 5 with B and pass through the single A at the next corner. Peyote 5 with B. Repeat from * once. Step up (**figure 15**).

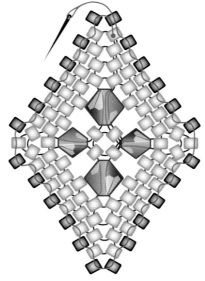

figure 15

Flat Rhombo Bead— Second Diamond

Make the second diamond like the first through row 5. Leave the thread attached.

Join the Diamonds

Add 2 Bs and pass through the next A at the north corner of the second diamond. Align the edges and zip the two diamonds together. When you reach the south corner, add 2 Bs, then continue zipping to the north corner.

Assemble

String the Large Rhombo Bead onto a head pin and trim the wire so that ⅜ inch (1 cm) extends beyond the bead. Make a small loop above the bead. String each Flat Rhombo Bead lengthwise onto an eye pin, trim as above, and make a small loop on the end of each bead.

Cut the chain into two 6½-inch (16.5 cm) sections and one 4-inch (10 cm) section. Attach the loop above the Large Rhombo Bead to the center link of the 4-inch (10 cm) chain. Attach one Flat Rhombo Bead to each end of the 4-inch (10 cm) chain. Attach one 6½-inch (16.5 cm) chain to the other end of each Flat Rhombo Bead. Use jump rings or split rings to attach the clasp to each end of the chain.

SUPPLIES

Size 11° cylinder beads:

A (shown in green), 2 g

B (shown in yellow), 5 g

6 fuchsia 6-mm bicone crystals (Swarovski 5328)

6 fuchsia 4-mm bicone crystals (Swarovski 5328)

FireLine 6 lb

Size 10 beading needle

Microcrystalline wax

Scissors

Lighter

DIMENSIONS

1⅛ inches (2.8 cm) in diameter

First Diamond

With 2 yards (about 2 m) of thread in your needle, bring the ends together, wax well, knot, clip the tail close to the knot, and melt the ends slightly.

Rows 1–4: Follow the directions on page 75 for rows 1–4 of the Large Rhombo Bead's first diamond.

Row 5: *Add 2 As and pass through the next A at this corner. Peyote 4 with A. Add 1 A between the two As at the west corner. Peyote 4 with A. Repeat from * once. Step up.

Row 6: *Add 1 B and pass through the next A at this corner. Peyote 10 with B. Repeat from * once. Weave in the thread and clip.

Second Diamond

Rows 1–5: Follow the directions through row 5 for the Large Rhombo Bead's first diamond.

Row 6: Add 1 B and pass through the next A. Zip the next two sides to the two sides of the first diamond. Add 1 B at the south corner and continue to peyote the next two sides with B. Weave in the thread and clip.

Third Diamond

Rows 1–5: Follow the directions through row 5 for the first diamond.

Row 6: Add 1 B and pass through the next A. Zip the next two sides to the two sides of the second diamond. Add 1 B at the south corner. Pass the thread through an A bead so you can pass through the three B beads at the south corners. Zip the next two sides to the first diamond. Weave in the thread and clip.

Note: If you plan to stiffen this bead, pass a large darning needle through the three B beads at each end to make it easier to string the bead after it dries. Follow the instructions on page 14 for using floor polish to stiffen the bead.

Beaded by Jane Langenback

Beaded by Liana Magee

Beaded by Ann Gilbert

THREE-SIDED STRIPED SWIRL BEAD

This version of the swirl bead is made using three colors. Stitch each half of the bead, then zip the two halves together.

Note: These instructions make a medium-size bead. See the chart on page 81 to make a larger version.

Make the First Half

With 2 yards (about 2 m) of thread in your needle, bring the ends together, wax well, knot, clip the tail close to the knot, and melt the ends slightly.

Row 1: String 3 As and form a ring secured with a lark's head knot as follows: Push the beads to within 1 inch (2.5 cm) of the knot. Separate the strands between the beads and the knot. Pass the needle between the strands, tighten, then pass back through the last bead strung (**figures 1** and **2**). Don't allow the knot to slip inside a bead. Orient the work so you're working counterclockwise (lefties, work clockwise).

figure 1

figure 2

Row 2: *Add 1 A and 1 B and pass through the next A. Repeat from * two more times. Step up. These beads form the three corners of the triangle. Make sure the pairs of beads at each corner sit almost parallel to each other. Adjust them if necessary (**figure 3**).

figure 3

Row 3: *Add 1 A and 1 B and pass through the next B. Add 1 C, skip one bead in the row below, and pass through the next A. Repeat from * two more times. Step up (**figure 4**).

figure 4

Row 4: *Add 1 A and 1 B and pass through the next B. Peyote once with C and once with B. Repeat from * two more times. Step up (**figure 5**).

figure 5

Row 5: *Add 1 A and 1 B and pass through the next B. Peyote once with C, once with B, and once with C. Repeat from * two more times. Step up (**figure 6**).

figure 6

Begin the Curve

From now on, you'll repeat two rows until the first half of the bead is the desired size.

Note: The step up will always be at the same corner. If you're uncertain about seeing it, count out 3 As. When you've used them, the next corner is the step up.

Row 6: *Add 1 A and pass through the next B. Peyote along the side with C, B, C, and B. Repeat from * two more times. Step up. Your thread will be exiting a corner A (**figure 7**).

figure 7

Row 7: *Add 1 A and 1 B and pass through the next C. Peyote along the side with B, C, B, and C. After completing the last stitch, step up through the first A added in this row (**figure 8**).

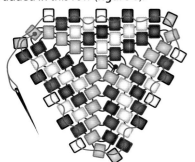

figure 8

General Rules for Swirl Beads

1 Color pattern for the sides

On row 3, the color pattern begins to develop when you add 1 C on each side. On subsequent rows the first bead on each side will be the same color as the one you will pass through next. The last bead on each side will be the opposite color of the previous bead added.

2 Zipping

For two edges of peyote stitch to zip together, one piece must have an additional row so beads on one edge will fit between beads on the opposite edge like a zipper.

Following this rule, if the Swirl Bead is worked with one half through row 12 and one half through row 11, the two halves will zip together perfectly because one half has one more "up" bead, and these "up" beads will mesh with the other half.

However, if the Swirl Bead is worked with one half through row 10 and one half through row 11, they will not zip together correctly because these rows have the same number of "up" beads on each side.

3 How to count rows

Starting from the center, count the A beads as shown in **figure 9**.

4 Changing size

To change the bead size, work each half using these row counts:

Small bead: First half, rows 1–10; second half, rows 1–9.

Medium bead: First half, rows 1–12; second half, rows 1–11.

Large bead: First half, rows 1–14; second half, rows 1–13.

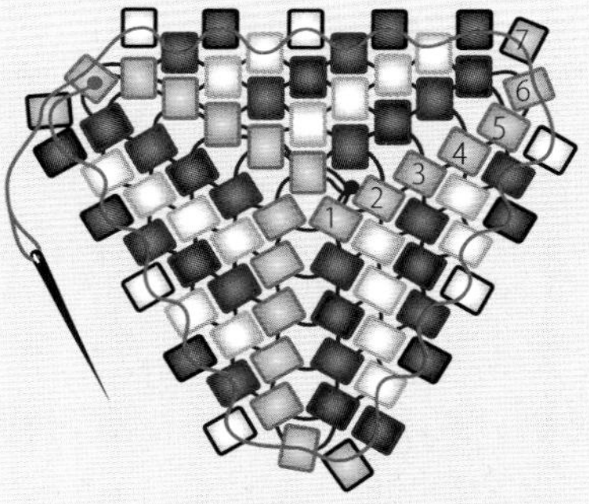

figure 9

5 Stiffening the bead

After zipping the halves together, weave in the thread, leaving a short length to hold on to if you wish to dip the bead into acrylic floor polish to stiffen it. To ensure having an opening to string the bead, push a heavy needle through the center of the three beads in row 1 on each side.

Note: After row 7, the A beads will begin to curve. Keep your tension tight so that the piece begins to cup.

Continue stitching following the chart below until you complete 12 rows. Row 8 will look like **figure 10**.

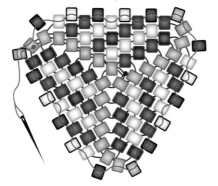

figure 10

Join the Two Halves

The first half of the bead should have 12 rows (or more if you're making a larger bead). Refer back to **figure 9** for how to count rows.

On the second half, complete row 11. After stepping up, your thread should be exiting an A bead at a corner (this corner has one AB pair). Position the two halves as shown in **figure 11** so the spirals are mirror images of each other and the stripes are aligned.

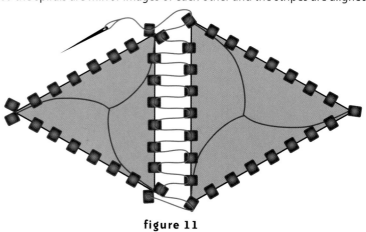

figure 11

Pass through the single A bead at a corner of the 12-row triangle, then through the B bead at the corner of the 11-row triangle just exited.

Continue to zip the two halves together, matching the stripes. At each corner, the single A from the 12-row triangle will sit between the AB pair at a corner on the 11-row triangle.

Swirl Bowls

These are half of a swirl bead made with size 11° or size 8° seed beads.

Multicolor Stripe

Follow the basic instructions, but use the chart below.

Work with four colors: A, the swirl color (shown in red), and B (blue), C (green), and D (yellow), which are the stripes.

Make the first half of the bead following rows 1–14. Weave in the thread and clip. Make the second half following rows 1–13. For a bead ¾ inch (2 cm) in diameter, work the first half with rows 1–12 and the second half with rows 1–11.

For a larger bead, work the rows as follows:

	Corners	Sides	Beads/Side
Row 1:	3A	-	0
Row 2:	AD	-	0
Row 3:	AB	D	1
Row 4:	A	BD	2
Row 5:	AC	BD	2
Row 6:	A	CBD	3
Row 7:	AD	CBD	3
Row 8:	A	DCBD	4
Row 9:	AC	DCBD	4
Row 10:	A	CDCBD	5
Row 11:	AB	CDCBD	5
Row 12:	A	BCDCBD	6
Row 13:	AD	BCDCBD	6
Row 14:	A	DBCDCBD	7

Note: The spiral begins to turn on this pattern after row 4 as compared to row 6 in the previous pattern.

Three-Sided Swirl Bead Chart

The chart below shows the color pattern for the corners and sides and the number of beads per side. Work the first half of the swirl bead as in rows 1–12. Weave in the thread and clip. Work the second half through row 11, but leave the thread attached. Use it to zip the two halves together. Remember to step up at the end of each row. The step up always occurs at the same corner.

	Corners	Sides	Beads/Side
Row 1:	3A	-	0
Row 2:	AB	-	0
Row 3:	AB	C	1
Row 4:	AB	CB	2
Row 5:	AB	CBC	3
Row 6:	A*	CB x 2	4
Row 7:	AB	BC x 2	4
Row 8:	A	BC x 2 + B	5
Row 9:	AB	CB x 2 + C	5
Row 10:	A	CB x 3	6
Row 11:	AB	BC x 3	6
Row 12:	A	BC x 3 + B	7

*When adding a single A at a corner after row 6 where the curve begins, place it between the A and B beads at the corner of the previous row.

To make a larger bead, add the following two rows:

Row 13:	AB	CB x 3 + C	7
Row 14:	A	CB x 4	8

Chevron Pattern Variation

Photo by Nathalie Mornu

If you follow my instructions, the sides will look like the bead on the right. But if you turn the second half of the piece inside out before zipping, the stripes on each half form chevrons instead of continuous stripes along the sides.

Five-Spiral Swirl Bead

SUPPLIES

Size 11° seed beads:

A (shown in red), 1 g

B (shown in black), 1 g

C (shown in white), 1 g

Nymo D or FireLine 6 lb

Size 10 beading needle

Microcrystalline wax

Scissors

Lighter

DIMENSIONS

1 inch (2.5 cm) in diameter

Note: Color A beads form the main radiating swirl lines and should be the strongest color. Colors B and C form the stripes. For a larger bead, try substituting size 8° seed beads for the size 11° seed beads.

With 2 yards (about 2 m) of thread in your needle, bring the ends together, wax well, knot, clip the tail close to the knot, and melt the ends slightly.

Row 1: String 5 As and form a ring secured with a lark's head knot as follows: Push the beads to within 1 inch (2.5 cm) of the knot. Separate the strands between the beads and the knot. Pass the needle between the strands, tighten, then pass back through the last bead strung (**figures 1** and **2**). Don't allow the knot to slip inside a bead. Orient the work so you're working counterclockwise (lefties, work clockwise).

Row 2: *Add 1 A and pass through the next A. (Don't skip a bead.) Repeat from * four more times. Step up (**figure 3**).

Note: If you're concerned about missing the step up, count out 5 As. When you've used the 5 As, the next corner will be the step up.

Row 3: *Add 1 A and 1 B and pass through the next A. Repeat from * four more times. Step up (**figure 4**).

Row 4: *Add 1 A and pass through the next B at this corner. Add 1 C, skip one bead in the row below, and pass through the next A. Repeat from * four more times. Step up (**figure 5**).

Row 5: *Add 1 A and 1 B and pass through the next C. Add 1 C, skip one bead in the row below, and pass through the next A. Repeat from * four more times. Step up (**figure 6**).

Row 6: *Add 1 A and pass through the next B at this corner. Add 1 B, skip one bead in the row below, and pass through the next C. Add 1 C and pass through the next A. Repeat from * four more times. Step up (**figure 7**).

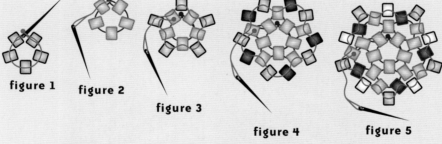

figure 1   **figure 2**

figure 3

figure 4   **figure 5**

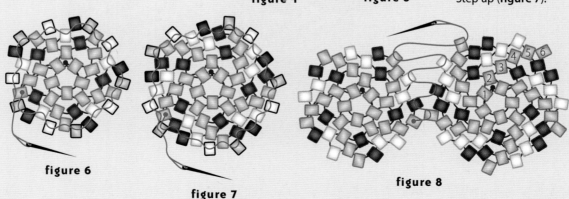

figure 6

figure 7

figure 8

Small Bead

Make the first half with eight rows (see chart below), ending with a single A at each corner. Weave in the thread and clip.

Make the second half with seven rows, ending with an AB pair at each corner. Turn the second half inside out.

With the thread exiting an A at a corner on the second half, pass through the single corner A bead of the first half, then back through the B at the same corner on the second half. Continue to zip around (**figure 8**). Weave in the thread and clip.

Note: In **figure 8**, the spirals go in opposite directions. The right piece shows how to count the rows.

Medium Bead

Make the first half with 10 rows and the second half with nine rows, using the chart below.

Large Bead

Using the chart below, make the first half with 12 rows and the second half with 11 rows.

	Corners	Sides	Beads/Side
Row 1:	5A	-	0
Row 2:	A	-	0
Row 3:	AB	-	0
Row 4:	A	C	1
Row 5:	AB	C	1
Row 6:	A	BC	2
Row 7:	AB	BC	2
Row 8:	A	CBC	3
Row 9:	AB	CBC	3
Row 10:	A	BC x 2	4
Row 11:	AB	BC x 2	4
Row 12:	A	CBCBC	5

In this necklace, A is black, B is bronze, and C is red. The necklace consists of seven large beads, two medium beads, and two small beads. Each bead is attached to the strand through the bead at the tip of a spiral.

Understanding This Pattern

This is another way to think about it.

Odd-numbered rows At each corner, add the 1 A/1 B pair and pass through the next "up" bead. Then peyote to the next corner, always adding the bead color opposite the one you will pass through next. The last bead on each side will be the opposite color of the last bead added.

For example, after you add an AB pair at a corner and pass through the next "up" bead, add a B if the next bead is a C. If the next color is a B, then add a C.

Even-numbered rows Add 1 A between the AB pair in the previous row, then peyote to the next corner, always adding the bead color opposite the one you are going into. At the end of the side, the last bead will be the color opposite of the last color.

SUPPLIES

Size 11° cylinder beads:

A (shown in dark gray), 2 g

B (shown in green), 3 g

C (shown in red), 2 g

Nymo D or FireLine 6 lb

Size 10 beading needle

Microcrystalline wax

Scissors

Lighter

DIMENSIONS

2 inches (5 cm) in diameter

PEEKABOO SOCCER BALL BEAD

This bead is the shape of the familiar black-and-white soccer ball. Also known as a Buckyball (after R. Buckminster Fuller, who designed the geodesic dome), its formal name is truncated icosahedron.

Overview

The shape contains 20 hexagons and 12 pentagons (**figure 1**). Please read the instructions before making any hexagons and pentagons.

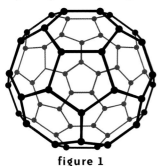

figure 1

First Half

Note: In the figures below, pentagons are shown in gray, hexagons in black.

Make one pentagon as described in the box at right. After completing row 3, peyote around all five sides with C. These are the connector beads. Weave in the thread and clip.

*Make one hexagon as described in the box. After completing the hexagon, align the corners and zip it to one side of the first pentagon. Weave in the thread and clip. Repeat from * four more times (**figure 2**).

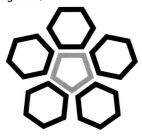

figure 2

Pentagons

With 2 yards (about 2 m) of thread in your needle, bring the ends together, wax well, knot, clip the tail close to the knot, and melt the ends slightly.

Row 1: String 20 As and form a ring secured with a lark's head knot, as follows: Push the beads to within 1 inch (2.5 cm) of the knot. Separate the strands between the beads and the knot. Pass the needle between the strands, tighten, then pass back through the last bead strung (**figure A**). Don't allow the knot to slip inside a bead. Orient the work so you're working counterclockwise (lefties, work clockwise).

figure A

Row 2: *Peyote once with B. Add 2 Bs and pass through the second A, counting from where the thread exits a bead. Repeat from * five more times. Step up (**figure B**).

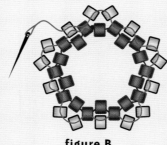

figure B

Row 3: Peyote around with B, adding one B over each single bead and between each pair of beads in the previous row (**figure C**). Leave the thread attached.

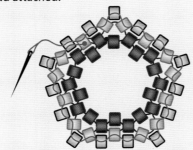

figure C

Hexagons

Row 1: String 24 As and form a ring secured with a lark's head knot, as described in Row 1 of Pentagons. Pass back through the last bead strung (**figure D**).

figure D

Row 2: *Peyote once with B. Add 2 Bs and pass through the second A. Repeat from * four more times. Step up (**figure E**).

figure E

Row 3: Peyote around with B, adding 1 B over each single bead and between each pair of beads in the previous row (**figure F**).

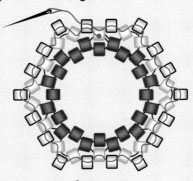

figure F

To zip the sides of the hexagons, anchor the thread so it exits a corner bead of one hexagon, as shown by the upper arrow in **figure 3**. Add connector beads using C along the straight lines on four sides of the first hexagon, then zip the first hexagon to the second along the dotted line. Repeat this step to connect the next four hexagons.

figure 3

*Make one pentagon. After completing row 3, add connector beads around three sides with C. Zip the two remaining sides between two hexagons. Weave in the thread and clip. Repeat from * four times as shown in **figure 4**.

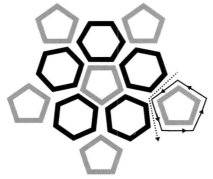

figure 4

*Make one hexagon, adding connector beads on three sides. Zip the three remaining sides to a pentagon, a hexagon, and another pentagon. Weave in the thread and clip after adding each one. Repeat from * four times as shown in **figure 5**.

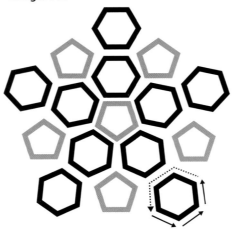

figure 5

Second Half

Repeat the instructions for the first half of the soccer ball, but don't add connector beads around the outside of the pentagons or the hexagons (just pass through beads to the next corner) when you make the second half.

Zip the two halves together with the hexagons of one half joined to the pentagons of the other half. At the corners, pass through the three corner beads in a circular fashion, then continue zipping.

Weave in the thread. (Leave a short length of thread to hold on to if you plan to dip the bead into acrylic floor polish to stiffen it.)

Variation

Beaded by Liana Magee

SUPPLIES

Size 11° cylinder beads:

A (shown in yellow), 2 g

B (shown in teal), 3 g

C (black), 2 g

**20 8-mm round crystals
(Swarovski 5000)**

**12 6-mm round crystals
(Swarovski 5000)**

FireLine 6 lb

Size 10 beading needle

Microcrystalline wax

Scissors

Lighter

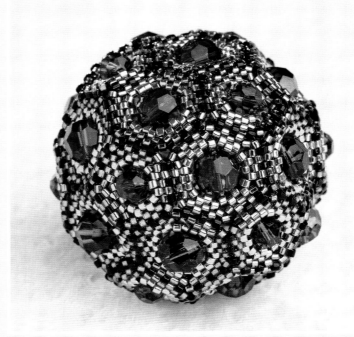

Make this variation following the directions for the Peekaboo Soccer Ball Bead, but add 8-mm crystals to the center of the hexagons and 6-mm crystals to the pentagons.

Add Crystals to Hexagons

After completing a hexagon as described on page 87, stitch through to any "down" bead in row 1, add one 8-mm crystal, and pass through a "down" bead (a "down" bead is a bead closest to the center) on the opposite side of row 1. Pass forward (enter the bead from the opposite side the thread exited) through the crystal and the bead exited at the beginning of this step. Weave in the thread and clip (**figure 6**).

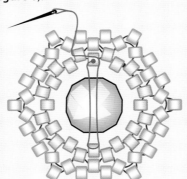

figure 6

Add Crystals to Pentagons

After completing a pentagon as described on page 87, stitch through to any "down" bead in row 1, add one 6-mm crystal, and pass through the "down" bead on the opposite side of row 1. Pass forward (enter the bead from the opposite side the thread exited) through the crystal and the bead exited at the beginning of this step. Weave in the thread and clip (**figure 7**).

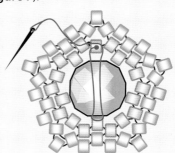

figure 7

Assemble

Assemble the Soccer Ball Bead Variation with Crystals following the directions for the Peekaboo Soccer Ball Bead on page 88.

Crayon Colors Necklace

The beaded beads in this necklace are dodecahedrons made up of 12 pentagons. To make these beads, follow the directions for adding crystals to pentagons on page 89 and assemble them like the Tiny Dodeca Bead on page 65.

Variation

A single bead with a pearl in the center of each pentagon.

Variation

One half of a soccer ball with crystals makes a festive bowl that can hold a single foil-wrapped chocolate or other tiny things.

SNUB CUBE BEAD

This three-dimensional shape is made up of triangles and squares.

SUPPLIES

Size 11° cylinder beads:

  A (shown in red), 2 g

  B (shown in yellow), 2 g

  C (shown in blue), 2 g

  D (shown in dark gray), 1 g

Nymo D or FireLine 6 lb

Size 10 beading needle

Microcrystalline wax

Scissors

Lighter

DIMENSIONS

1½ inches (3.8 cm) in diameter

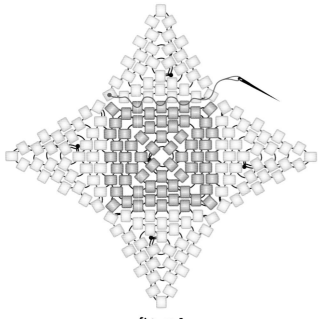

figure 1

1 Make six squares with A, working rows 1–6 of the square for the Pillow Bead on page 60. Weave in the thread and clip after completing each one.

2 Make eight triangles with C, working rows 1–4 of the triangle in the Cornerless Cube Bead on page 62. Weave in the thread and clip after completing each one.

3 Make four triangles with B as above, using 2 yards (about 2 m) of thread for the fourth triangle. Zip each triangle to one side of a square (**figure 1**). Weave in the thread and clip after completing each one except the fourth. Leave that thread attached.

4 Continuing with the thread from the fourth triangle, add 3 Ds to the outer edges of each of the four triangles as connector beads (**figure 2**). We'll now call this Unit A. Weave in the thread and clip.

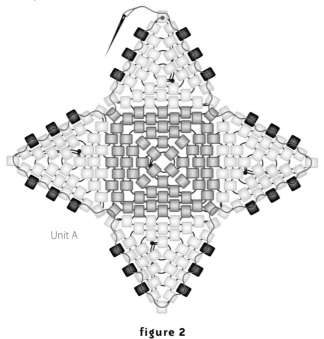

Unit A

figure 2

5 Zip one blue triangle to the edge of a yellow triangle on Unit A as shown in **figure 3**. Pass through the corner bead of the blue triangle and add 3 Ds as connector beads to the next side only (**figure 4**).

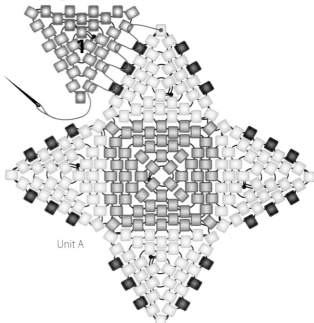

Unit A

figure 3

Unit A

figure 4

6 Zip a yellow triangle between the blue triangle just added and the next yellow triangle. At the corner pass through the corner bead of the yellow triangle and the square (**figures 5** and **6**). Pass through the tip bead of the new yellow triangle.

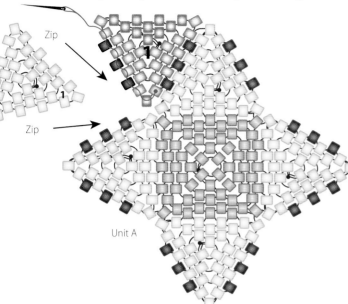

figure 5

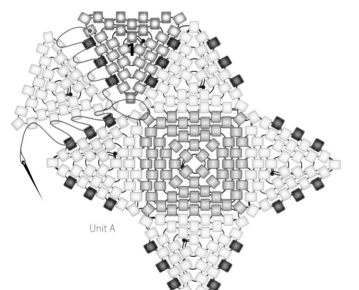

figure 6

7 Repeat steps 5 and 6 three times, adding three more blue triangles and three more yellow triangles to Unit A (**figure 7**). Weave in the thread and clip.

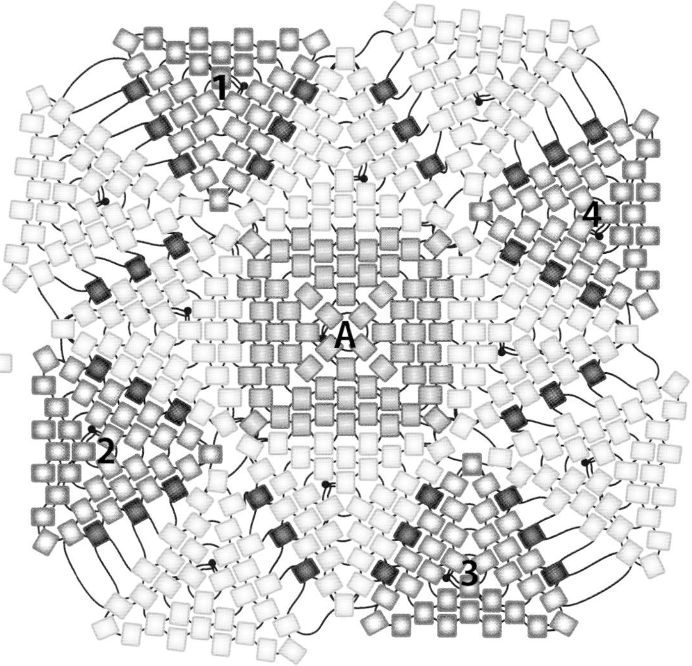

figure 7

The piece should now be domed and look like **figure 8**.

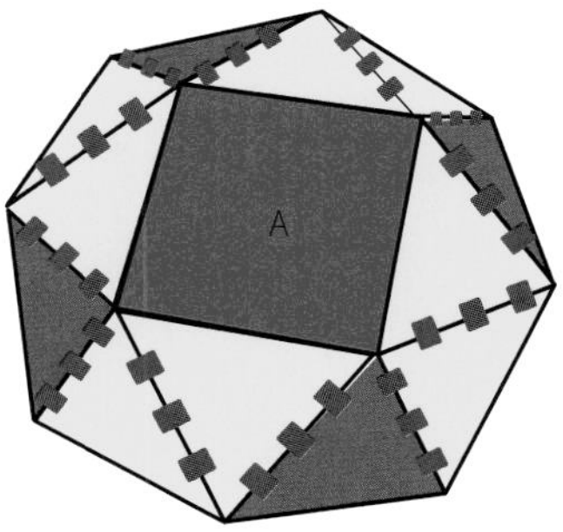

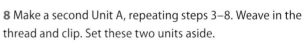

figure 8

8 Make a second Unit A, repeating steps 3–8. Weave in the thread and clip. Set these two units aside.

9 Begin a strip of squares and triangles that will connect the two Unit As as follows: Make a yellow triangle and attach it to a red square. Add 3 Ds as connector beads to the two outer edges of the triangle (**figure 9**). Weave in the thread and clip.

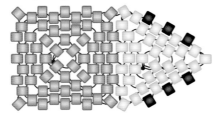

figure 9

10 Make a yellow triangle and zip it to a square on the side opposite the first yellow triangle. Add 3 Ds as connector beads to one side of this triangle, as shown in **figure 10**. Leave the thread attached.

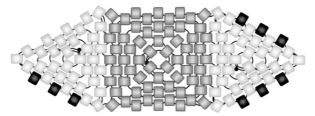

figure 10

11 Make three more two-triangle units as described in steps 9 and 10.

12 Zip the four units together as shown in **figure 11**. Zip the last unit to the first unit to make a ring. Clip the thread after joining the first three, but not after forming the ring.

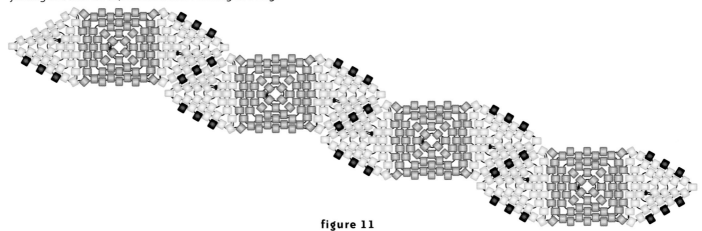

figure 11

13 Zip this ring to Unit A as follows: Zip the squares in the ring to the yellow triangles on Unit A; zip the yellow triangles in the ring to the blue triangles on Unit A (**figure 12**).

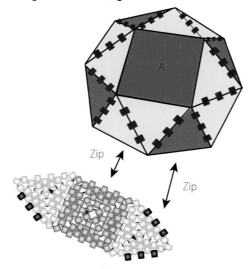

figure 12

14 Zip the opposite side of the ring to the second Unit A as in step 13 (**figure 13**). Weave in the thread. (Leave a short length of thread to hold on to if you plan to dip the bead in acrylic floor polish to stiffen it.)

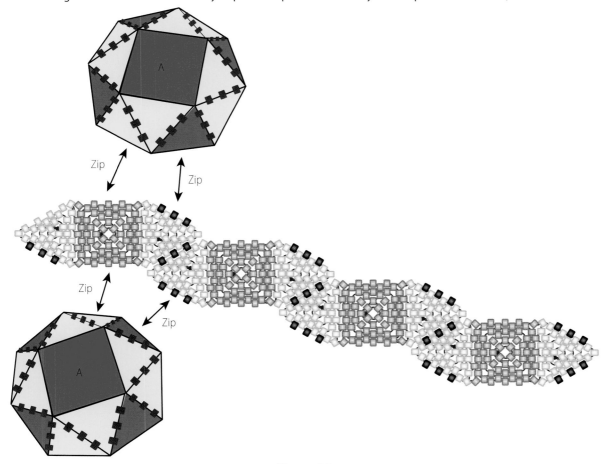

figure 13

Note: If you like the challenge of this bead, there are many others in the set known as the Johnson Solids. Images of these are available on the Internet.

Chapter 5
BEZELS

Shaped beadwork can be used to make bezels for rivolis and other fancy stones. These bezels can be used alone or attached to almost any shape.

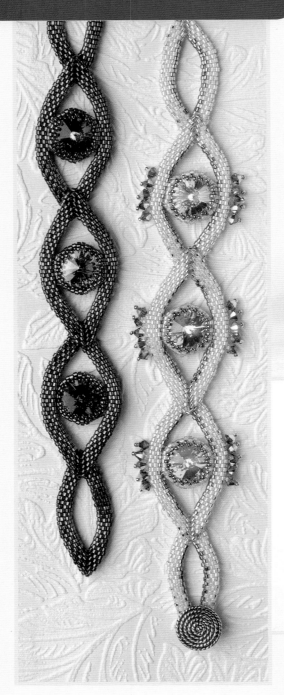

BASIC HEXAGON BEZEL

Because bezels with six sides have two straight opposing sides, they can easily be joined with rows of peyote stitch. This bezel is not only quick and easy to do, but it also gives a finished look to the reverse side of your beadwork and protects the rivoli from scratches.

SUPPLIES

Size 11° cylinder beads:

  A (shown in gray), 1 g

  B (shown in pink), 1 g

Size 15° Japanese seed beads:

  C (orange) < 1 g

1 black diamond 14-mm rivoli (Swarovski Art. 1122)

Nymo D or FireLine 6 lb

Size 10 beading needle

Microcrystalline wax

Scissors

Lighter

Note: When working these bezels, work with medium to soft tension until the last two or three rows. This makes it easier to sew into the bezel later if you are adding to it or sewing it to other beadwork.

Bezel for a 14-mm Rivoli

Note: Not every project in this chapter uses this style of bezel, but most do.

With 1½ yards (about 1.5 m) of thread in your needle, bring the ends together, wax well, knot, clip the tail close to the knot, and melt the ends slightly.

Row 1: String 6 As and form a ring secured with a lark's head knot as follows: Push the beads to within 1 inch (2.5 cm) of the knot. Separate the strands between the beads and the knot. Pass the needle between the strands, tighten, then pass back through

the last bead strung (**figure 1**). Don't allow the knot to slip into a bead. Orient the work so you're working counter-clockwise (lefties, work clockwise).

figure 1

Row 2: *Add 1 A and pass through the next A. Don't skip a bead. Repeat from * five more times. Step up (**figure 2**). These beads form the corners.

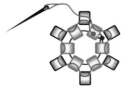

figure 2

Row 3: Peyote 6 around with B. Step up (**figure 3**).

figure 3

Row 4: *Add 2 As and pass through the next B. Repeat from * five more times. To form the piece into a cup, tighten the thread, and shape it over your finger. Step up (**figure 4**).

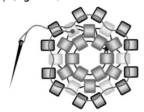

figure 4

Row 5: *Add 1 A and pass through the next A. Don't skip a bead. Peyote once with B. Repeat from * five more times. Step up (**figure 5**).

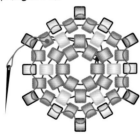

figure 5

Row 6: Peyote around with B. Step up.

Row 7: *Add 1 B and pass through the next B. Add 2 As and pass through the next B. Repeat from * five more times. Step up.

Row 8: Peyote around with B, adding 1 A between the 2 As at each corner. Step up.

Row 9: Peyote around with B. Step up.

Row 10: Peyote around with B. Step up. Insert the rivoli.

Rows 11 and 12: Peyote around with C. Step up. Weave in the thread and clip.

Bezel for a 16-mm Rivoli

Rows 1–9: Work as for rows 1–9 of the bezel for a 14-mm rivoli.

Row 10: Add 1 A at the corners and peyote around the sides with B. Step up.

Row 11: Peyote around with B. Step up. Insert the rivoli.

Row 12: Peyote around with B, adding 1 A above the As at the corners.

Rows 13 and 14: Peyote around with C. Tighten the thread to shape the bezel and secure the rivoli. Weave in the thread and clip.

Bezel for an 18-mm Rivoli

Rows 1–9: Work as for rows 1–9 of the bezel for a 14-mm rivoli.

Row 10: Add 2 As at each corner and peyote the sides with B. Step up.

Row 11: Add 1 A between the 2 As at each corner and peyote the sides with B.

Row 12: Peyote around with B.

Row 13: Peyote around with B, adding 1 A above the A at each corner. Insert the rivoli.

Rows 14–16: Peyote around with C. Tighten the thread to shape the bezel and secure the rivoli. Weave in the thread and clip.

DIAMOND AND RIVOLI EARRINGS

Rivolis sparkle from within a diamond-shaped frame, giving contrast of texture with their smooth finish. Dangle them from earrings or connect them for a necklace or bracelet.

SUPPLIES

Size 11° cylinder beads:

A (shown in yellow), 4 g

Size 15° Japanese seed beads:

B (shown in orange), < 1 g

2 heliotrope 12-mm rivolis (Swarovski 1122*)

2 thread protectors or wire guards (optional)

2 earring findings

Nymo D or FireLine 6 lb

Size 10 beading needle

Microcrystalline wax

Scissors

Lighter

Chain-nose pliers

* Or use a flat-back stone (such as Swarovski 2006).

DIMENSIONS

1⅛ x ¾ inches (2.8 x 2 cm)

Basic Diamond

With 2 yards (about 2 m) of thread in your needle, bring the ends together, wax well, knot, clip the tail close to the knot, and melt the ends slightly.

Note: In these instructions the corners are referred to as north, south, east, and west, as shown in **figure 1**.

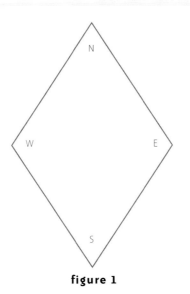

figure 1

Row 1: String 4 As and form a ring secured with a lark's head knot as follows: Push the beads to within 1 inch (2.5 cm) of the knot. Separate the strands between the beads and the knot. Pass the needle between the strands, tighten, then pass back through the last bead strung (**figure 2**). Don't allow the knot to slip into a bead. Orient the work so you're working counter-clockwise (lefties, work clockwise).

figure 2

Row 2: *Add 2 As and pass through the next A. Repeat from * three more times. Step up (**figure 3**).

figure 3

Note: The step up will always occur at the north corner.

Row 3: *Add 2 As and pass through the next A at the north corner. Don't skip a bead. Peyote once with A. Add 1 A between the pair at the corner. Peyote once with A. Repeat from * once. Step up (**figure 4**).

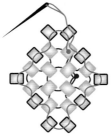

figure 4

Row 4: Add 2 As and pass through the next A at the north corner. Peyote 4 with A, passing through the single A at the west corner. Add 2 As and pass through the next A at the south corner. Peyote 4 with A, passing through the single A at the east corner. Step up (**figure 5**).

figure 5

Row 5: *Add 2 As and pass through the next A. Peyote twice with A. At the next corner, add 2 As above the single A added in row 3 and pass through the next A. Peyote twice with A. Repeat from * once. Step up (**figure 6**).

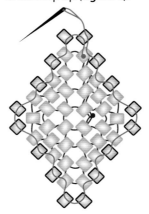

figure 6

Row 6: *Add 2 As and pass through the next A. Peyote 3 with A. At the next corner, add 1 A between the pair at the corner. Peyote 3 with A. Repeat from * once. Step up (**figure 7**).

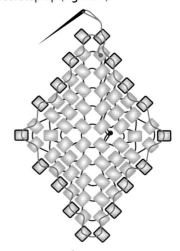

figure 7

Row 7: *Add 2 As and pass through the next A. Peyote 8 with A. Repeat from * once. Step up.

Row 8: *Add 2 As and pass through the next A. Peyote 4 with A. At the next corner, add 2 As above the single A added in row 6 and pass through the next A. Peyote 4 with A. Repeat from * once. Step up.

Row 9: *Add 1 B and pass through the next A. Peyote 5 with B. At the next corner, add 1 B between the pair at the corner. Peyote 5 with B. Repeat from * once.

Assemble

To add the thread protector, exit the B at the north corner, then pass through the thread protector and the next B. Weave in the thread and clip. If you aren't using thread protectors, add a loop of 8 Bs to connect the diamond to the earring finding.

With pliers, open the loop on the earring finding, insert the thread protector or loop of beads, and close the loop.

Bezel

Row 1: String 1 B and 1 A 14 times. Form a ring secured with a lark's head knot as follows: Push the beads to within 1 inch (2.5 cm) of the knot. Separate the strands between the beads and the knot. Pass the needle between the strands, tighten, then pass back through the last bead strung. Don't allow the knot to slip into a bead. Orient the work so you're working counterclockwise (lefties, work clockwise).

Row 2: Work one row of peyote stitch with A. Pull tight so the ring begins to form a tube. Step up.

Row 3: Repeat row 2. Step up.

Attach the Bezel to the Diamond

Center the bezel on the diamond with the B beads on top. Stitch the bezel to the diamond by passing back and forth through A beads in the diamond and A beads on the bezel. You may have to pass through the diamond as if you were taking a stitch in fabric. Your thread may pass around another thread or through a bead.

When you're halfway around, insert the rivoli between the bezel and the diamond, then continue to attach the bezel to the diamond.

Repeat all steps to make a second earring.

Diamonds with Rivolis Necklace

SUPPLIES

Size 11° cylinder beads:

  A, 12 g

Size 15° Japanese seed beads:

  B, 5 g

15 crystal celadon 12-mm rivolis (Swarovski 1122)

Clasp

Nymo D or FireLine 6 lb

Size 10 beading needle

Microcrystalline wax

Scissors

Lighter

DIMENSIONS

17½ inches (44.5 cm)

Diamond shapes, a classic in jewelry, are linked to create this necklace. Make 15 diamonds as for the Diamond and Rivoli Earrings on page 99, with this change: As you make each diamond after the first one, connect it to the previous diamond using the bead from the north or south corner as the tip bead in row 9. In other words, the diamonds share the size 15° seed beads at their north and south corners.

Diamond Bezel Earrings

Want to try a different approach to attaching the rivolis? These earrings enclose the crystal rivolis between two layers of diamonds.

SUPPLIES

Basic Beading Kit (see page 11)

Size 11° cylinder beads

    color A, 4 g

Size 15° seed Japanese seed beads, .5 g

2 14mm rivolis (Art. 1122)*

2 thread protectors (optional) (also called wire guards)

Earring findings

Nymo D or FireLine 6 lb

Size 12 beading needle

Microcrystalline wax

Scissors

Lighter

Chain-nose pliers

DIMENSIONS

1½ x ⅞ inch (3.8 x 2.2 cm)

Back Layer

Make the Basic Diamond on page 99 working rows 1-7. Then continue with rows 8 and 9:

Row 8: *Add 2 As and pass through the next A. Peyote 4 with A. At the west corner add 2 As above the single A added in row 6 then pass through the next A. Peyote 4 with A. Repeat from * once. Step up.

Row 9: *Add 2 As and pass through the next A. Peyote 5 with A. Add 1 A between the 2 A at the corner. Peyote 5 with A. Repeat from * once.

Weave in the thread and clip.

Front Layer

Prepare thread as for the Basic Diamond.

Row 1: String on 32 As and form a ring secured with a lark's head knot as follows: Push the beads to within 1 inch (2.5 cm) of the knot. Separate the strands between the beads and the knot. Pass the needle between the strands, tighten, then pass back through the last bead strung (figure 1). Don't allow the knot to slip into a bead. Orient the work so you're working counterclockwise (lefties, work clockwise).

Row 2: *Add 2 As, skip a bead, and pass through the next bead along the ring. Peyote 7. Repeat from the * once. Step up (figure 2).

Row 3: *Add 2 As and pass through the next A. Don't skip a bead. Peyote 8 with A. Repeat from the * once. Step up (figure 3).

Row 4: *Add 2 As and pass through the next A. Peyote 4 with A. Add 2 A and pass through the next A. Peyote 4 with A. Repeat from the * once. Step up.

Row 5: *Add 2 A and pass through the next A. Peyote 5. Add 1 A between the pair of A, then peyote 5. Repeat from the * once. Step up.

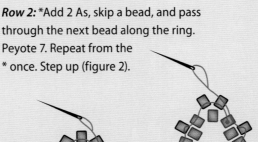

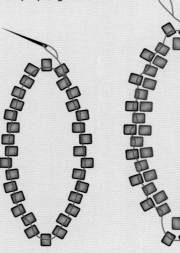

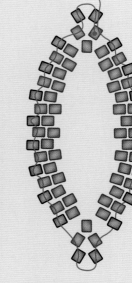

figure 1   figure 2   figure 3

Row 6: *Add 1 A and pass through the next A. Don't skip a bead. P 12-with A. Repeat from the * once. Step up.

Weave back to row 1 and P 14 with 15º seed beads around the bezel opening, adding only 1 15º at the north and south corners.

Joining the Layers

Weave through beads and exit the bead at the north corner of the diamond's front layer. Pass through the first bead of the pair at the north corner of the back layer, then through the single bead on the front layer. Continue to zip the edges together halfway around. Slip the rivoli between the two layers, then finish zipping around.

Add Edge Accents

With your thread exiting a bead at the north corner, "stitch in the ditch" (see Basics, page 14) to add B beads to the edge. To stitch in the ditch, add 1 B, then pass through the next bead in the row along the zipped edge. Don't add a B at the north corner. At the south corner, add a B, then pass forward through the single bead again.

Assemble

When the thread is again exiting the north corner, add the thread protector or a loop of 8 Bs, and pass through the single bead at the tip of the diamond again. Knot, weave in the thread, and clip.

With a pliers, open loop of the earring finding, insert the thread protector or loop of beads and close the loop. Repeat all steps to make a second earring.

Diamond Pendant Variation with Square Stitch Bail

This pendant is slightly larger than the diamond in the Diamond and Rivoli Earrings on page 99 and features a bail worked in square stitch.

SUPPLIES

Size 11° cylinder beads:

A, 4 g

Size 15° Japanese seed beads:

B, < 1 g

1 amethyst 14-mm rivoli (Swarovski 1122)

Nymo D or FireLine 6 lb

Size 10 beading needle

Microcrystalline wax

Scissors

Lighter

DIMENSIONS

1¾ x 1 inch (4.5 x 2.5 cm)

Diamond

Work rows 1–8 of the Basic Diamond on page 99, then repeat rows 6–9 once. When you stitch row 9, use 2 As at the north corner and 1 B at the east, west, and south corners and the sides.

Square Stitch Bail

After completing row 9 and stepping up at the north corner, work a 13-row square stitch strip, as follows:

*Add 2 As and pass through the next A. Don't skip a bead. Pass through the bead exited at the start of this step and the new bead added on the right (**figure 1**). Repeat from * 12 more times or to the desired length. Fold the strip to form a loop and attach the column to the pair of As at the top of the diamond.

figure 1

Bezel

Work the bezel following the directions on page 101, but start with 34 beads in row 1.

SUPPLIES

For a pair of earrings:

Basic Beading Kit

Cylinder beads, size 11º

    color A: 2 g

    color B: 2 g

Size 15º Japanese seed beads, 3 g

2 rivolis, 16mm (Art. 1122)

40 bugles, 3mm

40 bugles, 4mm

Earring findings

2 wire guards or soldered 3mm rings

DIMENSIONS

1.25 inches (2.8cm) diameter

BUGLE BURST EARRINGS

Lush with sparkle and framed with fringes of bugles, these earrings remind me of an opening flower.

1. Bugle Burst Earrings

Bezel the rivolis according to instructions for the Basic Hexagon Bezel for Rivolis for the 16mm rivoli on page 98.

Continuing with the same thread, exit a cylinder bead in row 12. Add 1 3mm bugle and 1 size 15º seed bead. Pass back through the bugle and through the next cylinder bead in this row (skip a bead in the row below like peyote stitch). Continue around the bezeled rivoli adding 20 bugles.

Pass through to exit a cylinder bead in row 11. Add 1 4mm bugle and 1 size 15º seed bead. Pass back through the bugle and through the next cylinder bead in this row (skip a bead in the row below like peyote stitch). Continue around the bezeled rivoli adding 20 bugles. These bugles will appear to fill in the space between the previous bugles.

Stitch through to exit a single corner bead in row 10. Pass through the wire guard or soldered ring and back through the cylinder bead. Repeat to reinforce, weave in the thread and clip.

Attach the earring finding: With a pliers, open the earring finding the place the wire guard or soldered ring in the opened loop. Close the loop.

Joining Bezeled Rivolis

Use the following instructions if you wish to join bezeled rivolis for a pendant or necklace.

Do not clip thread after completing the last row of the bezel. Pass thread through to the single corner bead in Row 11 to begin a strip of peyote six beads wide.

Row 1: Peyote across this side of the bezel adding three B and exiting the next corner bead of the bezel.

Row 2: Turn and peyote back across the row.

Rows 3-8: Continue peyote stitch back and forth for a total of 8 rows, then zip this strip to the next rivoli between the single corner beads of row 8.

To extend the length if necessary, make the peyote strips longer or shorter on each end, then attach the clasp.

Royal Jewels Necklace

Rivolis and fancy stones of various shapes and sizes form the components of this elegant necklace.

SUPPLIES

Size 11° cylinder beads:

    A (shown in gray), 3 g

    B (shown in purple), 8 g

Size 15° Japanese seed beads:

    C (shown in dark gray), 2 g

7 amethyst 16-mm rivolis (Swarovski 1122*)

12 silver 3-mm round beads

Two-strand clasp

Nymo D or FireLine 6 lb

Size 10 beading needle

Microcrystalline wax

Scissors

Lighter

* Or use a flat-back stone (such as Swarovski 2006).

DIMENSIONS

8 inches (20.5 cm)

TWO-LAYER HEXAGON BEZEL BRACELET

This bezel layers two hexagons with a rivoli sandwiched between them. They're joined using 3-mm beads.

Front Layer— Open Hexagon

With 2½ yards (about 2.5 m) of thread in your needle, bring the ends together, wax well, knot, clip the tail close to the knot, and melt the ends slightly.

Row 1: String 1 A and 5 Bs six times and form a ring secured with a lark's head knot as follows: Push the beads to within 1 inch (2.5 cm) of the knot. Separate the strands between the beads and the knot. Pass the needle between the strands, tighten, then pass back through the last bead strung (**figure 1**). Don't allow the knot to slip into a bead. Orient the work so you're working counterclockwise (lefties, work clockwise).

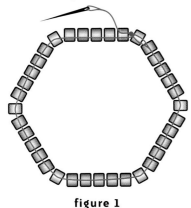

figure 1

Row 2: *Peyote twice with B, then add 2 As and pass through the next B. Repeat from * five more times. Step up (**figure 2**).

figure 2

Row 3: Add 1 A between the pairs of As at the corners and peyote the sides with B. Step up (**figure 3**).

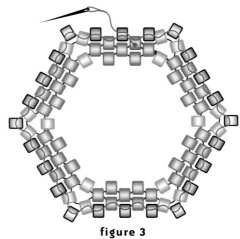

figure 3

Row 4: Peyote around with B, passing through the single A at each corner. Step up.

Row 5: Add 2 As at each corner and peyote the sides with B. Step up.

Row 6: Add 1 A between the pairs of As at the corners and peyote the sides with B. There will be 4 "up" B beads on each side, not counting the corner A beads.

Weave back to row 1 and peyote around the inner edge with C. At the corners above the A beads, add 2 Cs instead of 1 (**figure 4**). Weave in the thread and clip.

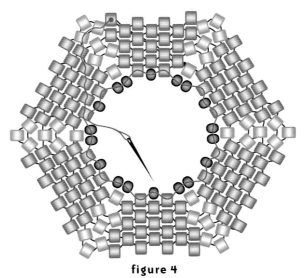

figure 4

Back Layer—Hexagon

Prepare the thread as above.

Row 1: String 6 As and form a ring secured with a lark's head knot as before. Pass back through the last A added (**figure 5**).

figure 5

Row 2: *Add 1 B and pass through the next A. Don't skip a bead. Repeat from * five more times. Step up (**figure 6**). These beads form the corners of the hexagon.

figure 6

Row 3: *Add 1 B and pass through the next A. Repeat from * five more times. Step up (**figure 7**).

figure 7

Row 4: *Add 2 As and pass through the next B. Repeat from * five more times. Step up through only the first bead of the pair (**figure 8**).

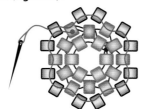

figure 8

Row 5: Add 1 A and pass through the next A. Don't skip a bead. Peyote once with B. Repeat from * five more times. Step up (**figure 9**).

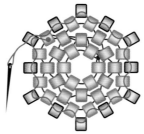

figure 9

Row 6: Peyote around with B. Step up (**figure 10**).

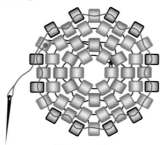

figure 10

Row 7: *Peyote once with B, then add 2 As above the A beads at the corner. Repeat from * five more times. Step up.

Row 8: Add 1 A between the A beads at each corner. Peyote twice on each side with B.

Row 9: Join the back layer to the front layer at each corner to hold the rivoli in place as follows: Pass through to the single A at a corner of row 8 on the bottom layer. Peyote the next side with B. After passing through the single A at the next corner, place the back layer on top of the front layer. Align the corners of row 3 on the front layer with the single corner A beads on row 8 of the back layer (which is now on top). Pass back through the single A on the front layer, then pass forward through the A just exited on the bottom layer (**figure 11**). Continue to peyote the sides of the back layer and join corner beads until you are halfway around. Then insert the rivoli and complete the row.

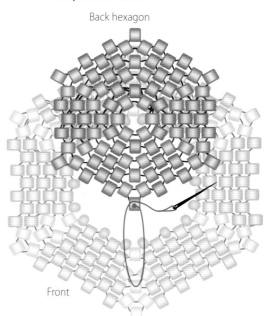

figure 11

Row 10: Add 2 As above the A beads at each corner. Peyote the sides with B. Step up.

Row 11: Add 1 A between the 2 As at each corner. Peyote the sides with B.

Row 12: Peyote around with B. Step up.

Row 13: Add 2 As above the A beads at each corner. Peyote three times on each side with B. Step up. There will be 3 "up" B beads between the A pairs on each side; the completed back layer will look like **figure 12**.

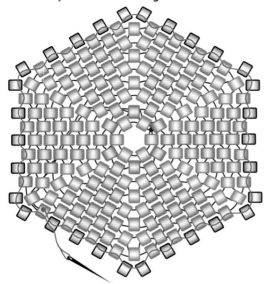

figure 12

Join the Layers

Zip the two layers together around the outer edge. The single A at each corner of the front layer fits between the pairs of A beads on the back layer (**figure 13**). Weave in the thread and clip.

Make six more bezels as described.

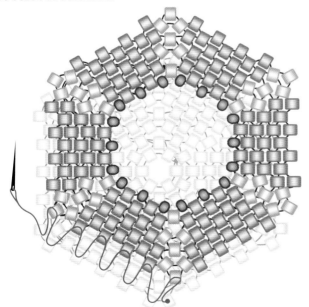

figure 13

Assemble

With the thread exiting the first B after a corner on the front layer, add one 3-mm round bead and pass through the same bead on the next hexagon. Pass back through the round bead and the bead exited on the first hexagon again. Pass through beads to the last B before the next corner. Repeat to add the second round bead (**figure 14**).

figure 14

Join the clasp to the bracelet just as you joined the units together, as shown in **figure 14**, with or without the round beads depending on the length desired. For extra length, add 3-mm beads between the clasp and the hexagon on each end.

SQUARE JASPER BRACELET

Frame square jasper stones with beaded bezels worked in circular and tubular peyote stitch. Make a decrease at each front corner to cinch the bezel around the stone.

SUPPLIES

Size 11° cylinder beads:

   A (shown in brown), 12 g

Size 15° Japanese seed beads:

   B (shown in light brown), 2 g

7 jasper 20-mm square stones

24 gold 3-mm round beads

Three-strand clasp

Nymo D or FireLine 6 lb

Size 10 beading needle

Microcrystalline wax

Scissors

Lighter

DIMENSIONS

8 inches (20.5 cm)

With 2 yards (about 2 m) of thread in your needle, bring the ends together, wax well, knot, clip the tail close to the knot, and melt the ends slightly.

Row 1: String 4 As and form a ring secured with a lark's head knot as follows: Push the beads to within 1 inch (2.5 cm) of the knot. Separate the strands between the beads and the knot. Pass the needle between the strands, tighten, then pass back through the last bead strung (**figure 1**). Don't allow the knot to slip into a bead. Orient the work so you're working counterclockwise (lefties, work clockwise).

figure 1

Row 2: *Add 1 A and pass through the next A. Repeat from * three more times. Step up (**figure 2**).

figure 2

Row 3: *Add 3 As and pass through the next A. Push down the middle bead of the three. Repeat from * three more times. Step up (**figure 3**). These beads form the corners of the square.

figure 3

Row 4: *Add 2 As and pass through the third A of the set of three beads at the corner. Add 1 A, skip 1 A in the row below, and pass through the next A. Repeat from * three more times. Step up (**figure 4**).

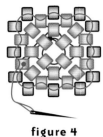

figure 4

Row 5: *Add 2 As and pass through the next A at this corner. Don't skip a bead. Peyote twice with A. Repeat from * three more times. Step up (**figure 5**).

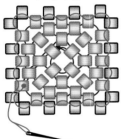

figure 5

Row 6: *Add 1 A and pass through the next A at this corner. Don't skip a bead. Peyote 3 with A. Repeat from * three more times. Step up (**figure 6**).

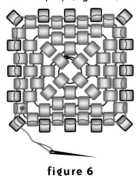

figure 6

Row 7: *Peyote 4 with A. Repeat from * three more times. Step up (**figure 7**). End by exiting the first bead after a single corner bead.

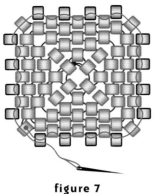

figure 7

Rows 8–13: Continue, following the chart below, which shows the number of beads at each corner and along each side:

Row	Corners	Sides
Row 8:	3	3
Row 9:	2	4
Row 10:	2	5
Row 11:	1	6
Row 12:	0*	7
Row 13:	1	6

* Where zero (no bead) is indicated at a corner, pass through the single corner bead in the previous row.

Note: Because the thickness of stones may vary, you may need to work extra rows of tubular peyote to make the height of the bezel tall enough to fit over the edge of the stone.

Row 14: *Peyote 5 with A. Add 1 A and pass back through the single bead at the corner in row 13. Then pass forward through the new A and the next

"up" bead (**figure 8**). Repeat from * three times. You'll have five "up" beads between corners when you complete this row. Pinch the corners to help form them into a square.

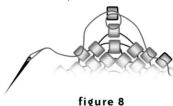

figure 8

Row 15: Place a 20-mm stone in the beadwork, then peyote around with A.

Row 16: Peyote around with B. Pull the thread toward the center to tighten the bezel. Weave in the thread and clip.

Repeat all steps to make a bezel for each of the other six stones.

Join the Bezeled Stones

With your thread exiting a corner bead on row 12, add one 3-mm bead and pass through the corner bead of the next square bezel. Pass back through the 3-mm bead, pass forward again through the corner bead exited at the beginning of this step, then pass through the 4 As along the edge. Add the next two 3-mm beads the same way (**figure 9**). Continue to connect the square bezels and add the clasp in the same way.

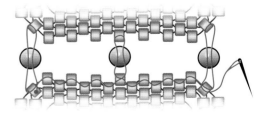

figure 9

Mancuff

SUPPLIES

Size 11° cylinder beads:

A (shown in blue), 4 g

B (shown in brown), 10 g

Size 15° Japanese seed beads:

C (orange), 1 g

3 heliotrope 14-mm rivolis
(Swarovski 1122)

Snap

Nymo D or FireLine 6 lb

Size 10 beading needle

Microcrystalline wax

Scissors

Lighter

DIMENSIONS

8 inches (20 cm)

MANCUFF AND M'LADY BRACELET

These two bracelets are made the same way, but one looks distinctly more feminine and the other more masculine. Only the colors and a tiny bit of embellishment make them different. The masculine bracelet, at left in the photo, has shapes that resemble copper tubing, and it closes with a snap. The feminine version looks like a bit of frothy confection with crowns of bicone fringes. For a clasp, the last pointed oval serves as the loop for a button.

Bezels

Bezel three 14-mm rivolis following the directions for the Basic Hexagon Bezel on page 97. Leave the thread attached to sew the rivolis in place.

Pointed Ovals with Bezeled Rivolis—First Layer

Work with medium-soft tension and keep the work flat. Don't pull tightly on the outer rows. Check off rows as you work.

With 2 yards (about 2 m) of thread in your needle, bring the ends together, wax well, knot, clip the tail close to the knot, and melt the ends slightly.

Row 1: String 1 A, 27 Bs, 4 As, 27 Bs, and 3 As and form a ring secured with a lark's head knot as follows: Push the beads to within 1 inch (2.5 cm) of the knot. Separate the strands between the beads and the knot. Pass the needle between the strands, tighten, then pass back through the last bead strung (**figures 1** and **2**). Don't allow the knot to slip inside a bead. Orient the work so you're working counterclockwise (lefties, work clockwise).

Row 2: *Add 2 As and pass through the next A. Don't skip a bead. Peyote the side with B. Repeat from * once. Step up (**figure 3**).

Row 3: Repeat row 2. There will be one more B on each side than on the previous row.

Row 4: Repeat row 2. There will be one more B on each side than on the previous row.

Row 5: Peyote around with A, adding only 1 A between the pairs of As at each point (**figure 4**).

Pointed Ovals with Bezeled Rivolis—Second Layer

Weave through A beads as shown in **figure 5**. Your thread will exit the lower A of the first pair on the first row.

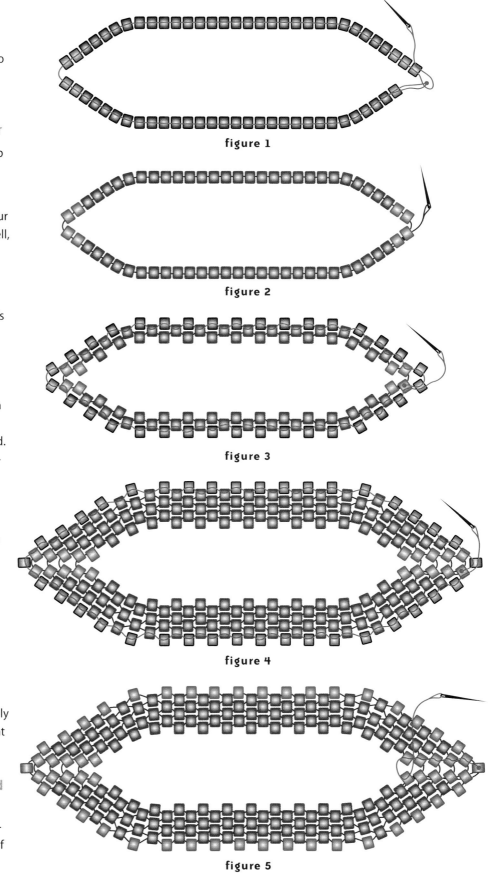

figure 1

figure 2

figure 3

figure 4

figure 5

Row 1: *Add 2 As and pass through the upper bead of the first pair on the upper side of the column (**figure 6**). Peyote 14 with B. Repeat from * once. Step up.

Note: This new pair will stand up slightly.

Rows 2–4: Add 2 As between the new pair of As at each point. Peyote the sides with B. Step up. There will be one more B on each side than on the previous row.

Attach the Rivoli

Center a bezeled rivoli in the oval and sew it to row 1.

Join the Outer Edges

Zip the second layer to the first layer along the outer edge. At the corners, pass through the first A on the second layer, the single bead at the tip of the first layer, then the next A on the second layer. Weave in the thread and clip.

Make a total of three pointed ovals with bezeled rivolis.

Pointed Ovals without Rivolis

Follow the directions above with this change: On row 1, begin with 1 A, 19 Bs, 4 As, 19 Bs, and 3 As.

Make a total of two pointed ovals without rivolis.

Assemble

Overlap the pointed ends as visible in the photo and sew the ovals together. Sew half the snap to each end as the clasp.

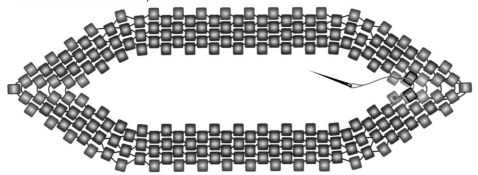

figure 6

M'Lady Bracelet

SUPPLIES

Size 11° cylinder beads:

  A (silver-lined green), 4 g

  B (cream), 10 g

  Gold, 2 g

Gold 15º seed beads, 1 g

3 ultra-lime 14-mm rivolis (Swarovski 1122)

30 4-mm Tanzanite AB-2X bicone ecrystals (Swarovski 4328)

1 shank button, ½-⅝ inch (1.3-1.5 cm)

Nymo D or FireLine 6 lb

Size 10 beading needle

Microcrystalline wax

Scissors

Lighter

DIMENSIONS

7½ inches (19 cm)

For the M'Lady Bracelet, work as for the Mancuff on page 113. To embellish the bracelet, attach five 3-mm bicone crystals above and below each bezeled rivoli. Sew a shank button to one end. The last pointed oval serves as the button loop.

Chapter 6
POINTED OVALS

This distinctive oval lends itself to variations in size, embellishment, and color. Add a round bead to the oval's center to create a dramatic "eye," stitch pairs of ovals together to form butterfly wings, or embellish the edges with a crystal fringe.

Size 11° cylinder beads:

    A (shown in red), < 1 g

    B (shown in green), < 1 g

Nymo D or FireLine 6 lb

Size 10 beading needle

Microcrystalline wax

Scissors

Lighter

BASIC POINTED OVAL

The pointed oval shape consists of one or two layers worked in even-count circular peyote stitch. A single-layer oval ends as shown in figure 5. To make the second layer, you'll work additional rows off the first row of beads strung. Then, zip the two layers together along the outer edge to complete the basic shape.

To change an oval's size, increase or decrease the number of beads in the first row by two beads per side, always working with an odd number of main-color beads. You can also change the total number of rows. Each additional row you stitch will increase the number of main-color beads by one bead on each side.

Work with medium-soft tension and keep the work flat. Don't pull tightly on the outer rows. Check off rows as you work.

Note: In the diagrams, new beads are outlined for clarity.

First Layer

With 2 yards (about 2 m) of thread in your needle, bring the ends together, wax well, knot, clip the tail close to the knot, and melt the ends slightly.

Row 1: String 1 A, 13 Bs, 4 As, 13 Bs, and 3 As and form a ring secured with a lark's head knot as follows: Push the beads to within 1 inch (2.5 cm) of the knot. Separate the strands between the beads and the knot. Pass the needle between the strands, tighten, then pass back through the last bead strung (**figures 1** and **2**). Don't allow the knot to slip into a bead. Orient the work so you're working counterclockwise (lefties, work clockwise).

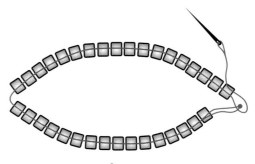

figure 1

figure 2

Row 2: *Add 2 As and pass through the next A. Don't skip a bead. Peyote 8 with B. Repeat from * once. Step up (**figure 3**).

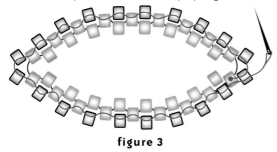

figure 3

Row 3: *Add 2 As and pass through the next A. Don't skip a bead. Peyote 9 with B. Repeat from * once. Step up.

Row 4: *Add 2 As and pass through the next A. Don't skip a bead. Peyote 10 with B. Repeat from * once. Step up.

Row 5: Peyote around with A, adding 1 A between the pairs of As at each point (**figure 4**).

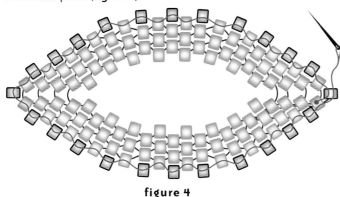

figure 4

Note: You can also work this row with size 8° drops or beads in a contrasting color.

Second Layer

Weave through A beads as shown in **figure 5**. Your thread will exit the lower A of the first pair on the first row.

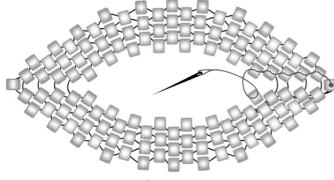

figure 5

Row 1: Add 2 As and pass through the upper bead of the first pair on the upper side of the column (**figure 6**). Peyote 7 with B. After exiting the A at the next point, add 2 As and pass through the A below it. Peyote 7 with B. Step up through the first A added in this row.

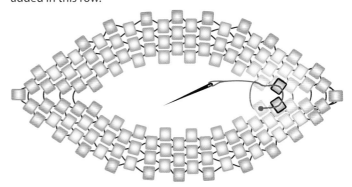

figure 6

Row 2: *Add 2 As between the new pair of As at this point. Peyote 8 with B. Repeat from * once. Step up.

Rows 3 and 4: Repeat row 2. There will be one more B on each side for each row.

Join the Outer Edges

Zip the second layer to the first layer along the outer edge. At the corners, pass through the first A on the second layer, the single bead at the tip of the first layer, and the next A on the second layer. Weave in the thread and clip.

Using a Chart

Once you understand how to make a Basic Pointed Oval, it's easy to make them in different sizes following a chart of the bead counts and colors for the corners and the sides. After stringing the first row of beads (in this case, 1 A, 13 Bs, 4 As, 13 Bs, and 3 As), work this bead sequence for the first layer:

Row	Corners	Sides
Row 2:	2 As	8 Bs
Row 3:	2 As	9 Bs
Row 4:	2 As	10 Bs
Row 5:	1 A	11 As

To stitch the second layer, weave through A beads to the first layer's starting row, as shown in **figures 5** and **6** above, and continue as follows:

Row	Corners	Sides
Row 1:	2 As	7 Bs
Row 2:	2 As	8 Bs
Row 3:	2 As	9 Bs
Row 4:	2 As	10 Bs

SUPPLIES

Size 11° cylinder beads:

A (shown in purple), 8 g

B (shown in pink), 12 g

Size 15° seed beads:

C (shown in yellow), 2 g

9 amethyst 8-mm round crystals (Swarovski 5000)

252 amethyst 3-mm bicone crystals (Swarovski 5328)

1 snap, 7 or 8 mm

FireLine 6 lb

2 size 10 beading needles

Microcrystalline wax

Scissors

Lighter

DIMENSIONS

7½ inches (19 cm)

PIRATE EYES BRACELET

Inspired by the eyes painted on Johnny Depp's face in *Pirates of the Caribbean: Dead Man's Chest*, I designed a bracelet that will become your swashbuckling favorite the moment you first wear it. In this variation of the pointed oval, you'll stitch an 8-mm round crystal into the oval's center before starting the second layer. A lavish crystal fringe embellishes the zipped edges of these intriguing "eyes."

Pointed Oval—First Layer

With 2 yards (about 2 m) of thread in your needle, bring the ends together, wax well, knot, clip the tail close to the knot, and melt the ends slightly.

Work the pointed ovals for this bracelet following the directions for the Basic Pointed Oval on page 116 but using the bead counts and colors shown in the chart below. Work with medium-soft tension and keep the piece flat. Check off rows as you work.

Row 1: String 1 A, 15 Bs, 4 As, 15 Bs, and 3 As.

	Corners	Sides
Row 2:	2 As	9 Bs
Row 3:	2 As	10 Bs
Row 4:	2 As	11 As
Row 5:	1 A	12 As

After completing row 5, set the needle and thread aside.

Add the Round Crystal

Prepare another needle and thread as described above with 12 inches (30 cm) of thread. Weave through beads and exit the eighth bead in the first row.

Add the round crystal, pass through the center bead on the opposite side, then pass back through the crystal. Pass through the eighth bead in the first row again, continue through the crystal, and exit the center bead on the opposite side (**figure 1**). Weave in the thread and clip.

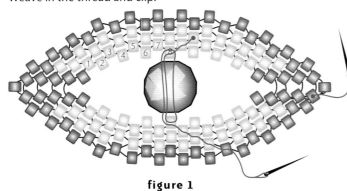

figure 1

Pointed Oval—Second Layer

Using the thread from the first layer, pass through the A beads at the pointed end and exit the lower A of the first pair in row 1 (**figure 2**).

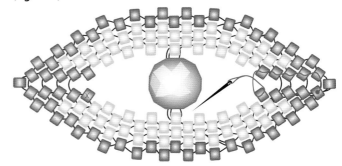

figure 2

	Corners	Sides
Row 1:	2 As	8 Bs
Row 2:	2 As	9 Bs
Row 3:	2 As	10 Bs
Row 4:	2 As	1 As

End row 4 exiting an A at the point.

Join the Outer Edges

Zip the second layer to the first along the outer edge (**figure 3**). At the corners, pass through the first A on the second layer, the single bead at the tip of the first layer, and the next A on the second layer. Weave in the thread and clip.

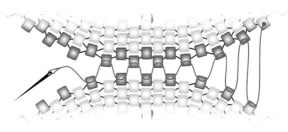

figure 3

Add Fringe

With 2 yards (about 2 m) of thread in your needle, prepared as above, exit an A bead in row 5 of the first layer.

Add a bicone and 1 C. Pass back through the bicone and pass through the next A on row 5. Repeat around the oval. At the points, pass through the single A and add a bicone and 1 C. Pass through the A again in the same direction (**figure 4**).

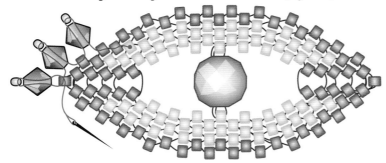

figure 4

Repeat these steps to make a total of nine pointed ovals.

Join the Ovals

Next, you'll make small rectangles in peyote stitch and use them to join the pointed ovals, as follows.

With 2 yards (about 2 m) of thread in your needle, prepared as before, exit the fourth bead from the right in the third row of the first layer, as shown in **figure 5**.

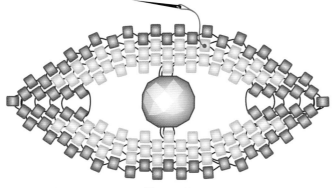

figure 5

Row 1: Peyote twice with B. Add 1 B, turn by passing under the thread between the next beads, and pass back through the last B (**figure 6**).

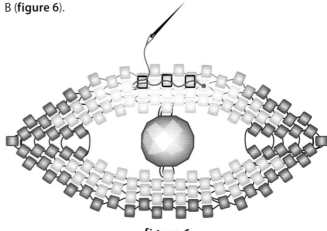

figure 6

figure 7

Row 2: Peyote twice with B (**figure 7**).

Row 3: Peyote twice with B. Still referring to **figure 7**, add 1 B, turn by passing the needle under the thread on the edge between the two previous rows, and pass back through the last B.

Rows 4–8: Continue until there are four beads on each side edge.

Stitch this end of the peyote strip to the corresponding beads on row 3 of another oval.

Assemble

Join all nine pointed ovals with peyote strips. For the clasp, stitch one strip on each end of the bracelet. Sew half of the snap to each of the peyote strips at the end.

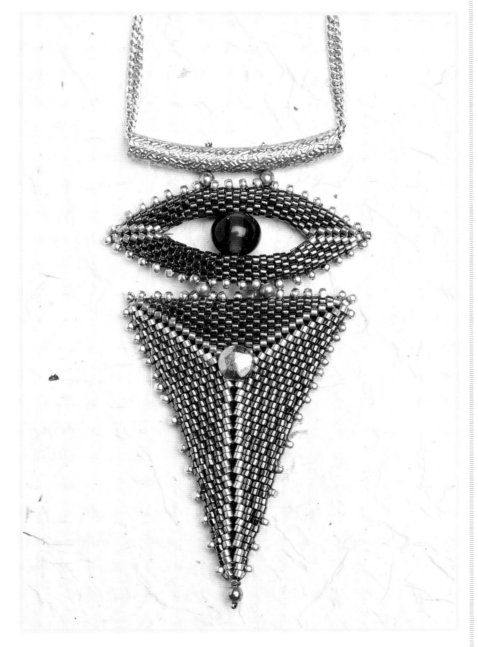

Size 11° cylinder beads:

A (shown in yellow), 2 g

B (shown in brown), 10 g

Size 11° seed beads:

C (shown in silver), 1 g

2 silver size 15° seed beads

5 silver 3-mm round metal beads

1 green 8-mm round glass bead

1 silver 40 x 5-mm curved metal tube bead

1 silver 7-mm nail head or shank button

Stiff felt, 4 x 4 inches (10.2 x 10.2 cm)

24 inches (61 cm) of chain, with clasp*

Nymo D or FireLine 6 lb

Size 10 beading needle

Microcrystalline wax

Scissors

Lighter

Drill with fine bit

* It will need to fit through the tubular bead.

DIMENSIONS

3½ x 2 inches (9 x 5 cm)

EYE-AND-TRIANGLE NECKLACE

This combination of elements—the lens shape and the isosceles triangle—creates a harmonious pendant suggestive of ancient hieroglyphics and the Egyptian Revival style of Art Deco jewelry.

Triangle—Front Layer

With 2½ yards (about 2.5 m) of thread in your needle, bring the ends together, wax well, knot, clip the tail close to the knot, and melt the ends slightly.

Row 1: String 3 As and form a ring secured with a lark's head knot as follows: Push the beads to within 1 inch (2.5 cm) of the knot. Separate the strands between the beads and the knot. Pass the needle between the strands, tighten, then pass back through the last bead strung (**figures 1** and **2**). Don't allow the knot to slip into a bead. Orient the work so you're working counterclockwise (lefties, work clockwise).

figure 1

figure 2

Row 2: *Add 2 As and pass through the next A on the ring.

• Add 4 As and pass through the next A.

• Add 2 As and pass through the next A. Step up. Make sure the holes in the beads at each corner are almost parallel. Adjust them if necessary (**figure 3**).

figure 3

Row 3: Add 2 As and pass through the next A.

• Add 1 B and pass through the next 2 As.

• Add 4 As and pass through the next 2 As.

• Add 1 B and pass through the next A.

• Add 2 As and pass through the next A.

• Add 1 B and pass through the next A. Step up (**figure 4**).

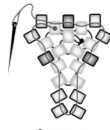

figure 4

Row 4: Add 2 As and pass through the next A.

• Add 1 B and pass through the next B.

• Add 2 Bs and pass through the next 2 As.

• Add 4 As and pass through the next 2 As.

• Add 2 Bs and pass through the next B.

• Add 1 B and pass through the next A.

• Add 2 As and pass through the next A.

• Peyote twice with B. Step up (**figure 5**).

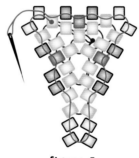

figure 5

Rows 5–15: Continue for another 11 rows, adding 2 As above the 2 As at the left and right corners and 4 As above the 4 As at the elongated point. Peyote the sides with B, adding 1 B above each single B and 2 Bs above each pair of Bs.

Sew the nail head to the front center at row 1.

Triangle—Back Layer

Repeat rows 1–15 of the front layer. Then stitch one more row with B, adding 1 A at each of the three corners.

Assemble

Cut a piece of felt slightly smaller than the triangle layers. Place it between the two layers and zip the layers together.

Hold the triangle with the elongated point down. Stitch around the outer edge with C, adding 1 A to the left and right corners as follows: Pass through the single A, add 1 C, and pass through the single A again in the same direction.

At the bottom point, add one 3-mm metal bead and 1 C. Pass back through the metal bead and continue through the A in the same direction.

Pointed Oval

Work the pointed oval for this pendant following the directions for the Basic Pointed Oval on page 116, with these changes:

First Layer

Row 1: String 1 A, 19 Bs, 4 As, 19 Bs, and 3 As.

	Corners	Sides
Row 2:	2 As	11 Bs
Row 3:	2 As	12 Bs
Row 4:	2 As	13 Bs
Row 5:	2 As	14 Bs
Row 6:	2 As	15 Bs
Row 7:	1 A	16 Bs

Attach the 8-mm bead after completing the first layer, following the directions for the Pirate Eyes Bracelet on page 119.

	Corners	Sides
Row 1:	2 As	10 Bs
Row 2:	2 As	11 Bs
Row 3:	2 As	12 Bs
Row 4:	2 As	13 Bs
Row 5:	2 As	14 Bs
Row 6:	2 As	15 Bs

Zip the outer edges together.

Assemble

Stitch the triangle to the pointed oval at two points, using two 3-mm metal beads between the triangle and the oval.

Drill two holes completely through the metal tube, about $\frac{9}{16}$ inch (1.4 cm) from each end and ½ inch (1.3 cm) apart. Center the chain in the metal tube.

Stitch the pointed oval to the tube through the drilled holes, using two 3-mm metal beads between the oval and the tube. After passing through the tube, add one size 15° seed bead and pass back through the tube and the metal bead. Repeat to reinforce the connection.

Cascade Necklace

SUPPLIES

Size 11° cylinder beads:

A (corner increases and outer edges), 5 g

B (main color), 18 g

Size 11° seed beads:

C (embellishment), 4 g

1 pin back, 1½ inches (4 cm) long

Nymo D or FireLine 6 lb

Size 10 beading needle

Microcrystalline wax

Scissors

Lighter

DIMENSIONS

3 x 2½ inches (7.5 x 6.5 cm)

OPERA HOUSE PIN

Inspired by the graceful vaulted shells that form the roof of the Sydney Opera House, this brooch consists of pointed ovals in graduated sizes that can be embellished with seed beads or crystals.

Stitch one each of the five pointed ovals described here, following the directions for the first layer of the Basic Pointed Oval on page 116, but with these changes to make them in graduated sizes:

Small Pointed Oval

Row 1: String 1 A, 13 Bs, 4 As, 13 Bs, and 3 As.

	Corners	Sides
Row 2:	2 As	8 Bs
Row 3:	2 As	9 Bs
Row 4:	2 As	10 Bs
Row 5:	1 A	11 As

Medium Pointed Oval

Row 1: String 1 A, 19 Bs, 4 As, 19 Bs, and 3 As.

	Corners	Sides
Row 2:	2 As	11 Bs
Row 3:	2 As	12 Bs
Row 4:	2 As	13 Bs
Row 5:	2 As	14 Bs
Row 6:	1 A	15 As

Large Pointed Oval

Row 1: String 1 A, 25 Bs, 4 As, and 25 Bs.

	Corners	Sides
Row 2:	2 As	14 Bs
Row 3:	2 As	15 Bs
Row 4:	2 As	16 Bs
Row 5:	2 As	17 Bs
Row 6:	2 As	18 Bs
Row 7:	1 A	19 As

Extra-Large Pointed Oval

Row 1: String 1 A, 31 Bs, 4 As, 31 Bs, and 3 As.

	Corners	Sides
Row 2:	2 As	17 Bs
Row 3:	2 As	18 Bs
Row 4:	2 As	19 Bs
Row 5:	2 As	20 Bs
Row 6:	2 As	21 Bs
Row 7:	2 As	22 Bs
Row 8:	1 A	23 As

Jumbo Pointed Oval

Row 1: String 1 A, 37 Bs, 4 As, 37 Bs, and 3 As.

	Corners	Sides
Row 2:	2 As	20 Bs
Row 3:	2 As	21 Bs
Row 4:	2 As	22 Bs
Row 5:	2 As	23 Bs
Row 6:	2 As	24 Bs
Row 7:	2 As	25 Bs
Row 8:	1 A	26 As

Second Layer

To start the second layer of each oval, pass through the corner beads and exit the first A on the lower side of the column of the inner row, following the directions for the second layer of the Basic Pointed Oval on page 117.

Following the chart above, begin each oval's second layer with row 2 of the first layer and don't work the last row of the first layer.

Zip the second layer to the first along the outer edge.

Embellishment

Using C, stitch in the ditch around the outer edge of each pointed oval. At the points, pass through the single A at the corner, add 1 C, then pass through the single A again in the same direction.

Join the Ovals

Stack the ovals with the smallest on top and the largest on the bottom so their bottom points are lined up over each other. Arrange the ovals as desired and stitch them together at the bottom points and on the sides where they overlap. Sew on the pin back as shown in the photo on page 124.

Opera Pin Variation with Crystal Fringe

SUPPLIES

Size 11° cylinder beads:

  A (corner increases and outer edges), 4 g

  B (main color), 15 g

Size 15° Japanese seed beads:

  C (embellishment), 2 g

144 smoke topaz AB 3-mm bicone crystals (Swarovski 5328)

1 pin back, 1¼ inches (3.5 cm) long

FireLine 6 lb

Size 10 beading needle

Microcrystalline wax

Scissors

Lighter

DIMENSIONS

2¾ x 2¼ inches (7 x 5.5 cm)

1 Make four ovals, small to extra-large, following the directions for the Opera House Pin.

2 Working along the last row of each pointed oval, replace the seed bead embellishment with crystal fringe, as follows: String one crystal and 1 C. Pass back through the crystal and through the next A on the last row on the outer

figure 1

edge. At the point, pass through the single A, then add a crystal and 1 C. Pass back through the crystal, then pass through the single A again in the same direction (**figure 1**). Continue to add crystals around the oval.

3 Assemble the embellished ovals and attach the pin back following the directions for the Opera House Pin.

SUPPLIES

Size 11° cylinder beads:

   A (shown in red), 5 g

   B (shown in brown), 4 g

   C (shown in green), 4 g

Size 15° Japanese seed beads:

   D (shown in orange), 2 g

1 red 20-mm round resin bead

72 yellow 2.5-mm bicone crystals (Swarovski 5328) or 2-mm round crystals or 2.8-mm drops

1 red 8-mm round crystal (Swarovski 5000)

1 red 6-mm bicone crystal (Swarovski 5328)

2 bead caps

1 head pin, 3 inches (7.5 cm) long

1 bail

FireLine 6 lb

Size 10 beading needles

Microcrystalline wax

Scissors

Lighter

Round-nose pliers

Wire cutters

DIMENSIONS

3 x 2½ inches (7.5 x 6.5 cm)

TROPICAL BAUBLE PENDANT

Is it a palm tree? A seedpod? An escapee from the *Little Shop of Horrors*? It looks like a plant form, but who knows?

Pointed Ovals

With 2½ yards (about 2.5 m) of thread in your needle, bring the ends together, wax well, knot, clip the tail close to the knot, and melt the ends slightly. Work with medium-soft tension and keep the piece flat. Leave the thread attached after completing each one.

Note: The pointed ovals in this bauble are joined to each other by zipping half of one oval to half of the next oval along the outer and inner edges, which is different from the technique shown in the Basic Pointed Oval on page 116. As you continue to connect the ovals this way, you'll form a pocket that surrounds the large resin bead.

Make six single-layer pointed ovals following the directions for the Basic Pointed Oval on page 116, but with the following changes:

Row 1: String 1 A, 19 Bs, 4 As, 19 Bs, and 3 As.

	Corners	Sides
Row 2:	2 As	11 Cs
Row 3:	2 As	12 Cs
Row 4:	2 As	13 Cs
Row 5:	2 As	14 Bs

Note: You'll have six pairs of A beads at each point and 14 "up" beads between points. Leave the thread attached to each oval.

First Pointed Oval *Only*—Inner Row

Pass through the pairs of A beads and exit the upper A of the first pair in row 1 (**figure 1**). Peyote 10 with D. Pass through 2 As at the second point. Peyote 10 with D. Pass through 6 As at the point (**figure 2**).

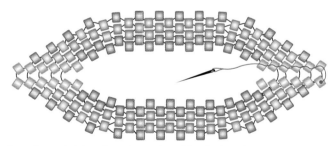

Pass through A beads to the center of the first oval.

figure 1

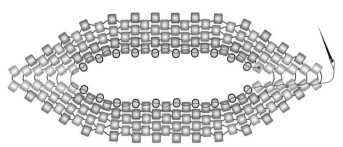

Add D beads around the inner row, then pass through A beads at the point.

figure 2

First Pointed Oval *Only*—Outer Row

*Add 1 A and pass through the next A at the point. Peyote 15 with A. Repeat from * once. Weave in the thread and clip (**figure 3**).

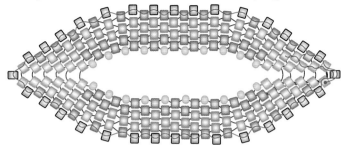

Add A beads at the points and around the edge, weave in the thread, and clip.

figure 3

Pointed Ovals—Second through Sixth Ovals

Join the second oval to the first one as follows: Pass through A beads to the second oval's inner row. Zip one edge on the inner row of the second oval to the corresponding edge on the inner row of the first oval, as shown in **figure 4**. Once the edges are

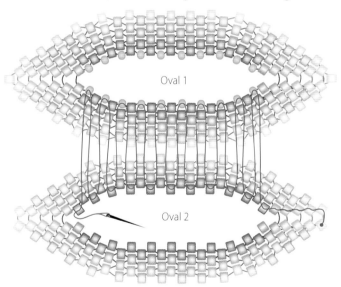

Zip the inner edge of the first oval to the inner edge of the second oval.

figure 4

zipped, add D beads to the remaining inner edge of the second pointed oval (**figure 5**).

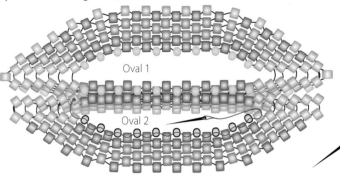

Add D beads to the inner edge of the second oval.

figure 5

How to hold the ovals when zipping the inner edges together.

Pass through A beads to the outer row. Add 1 A and pass through the next A at this point (**figure 6**).

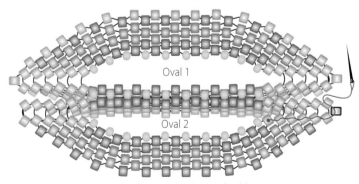

Pass through A beads to the outer edge and add 1 A.

figure 6

Zip the outer edge of the second pointed oval to the outer edge of the first oval above the zipped Ds (**figure 7**). Add a single A to the corner and peyote with A along the outer edge of the second pointed oval (**figure 8**).

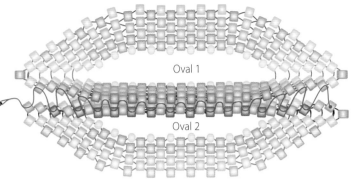

Zip the outer edge of the first oval to the outer edge of the second oval.

figure 7

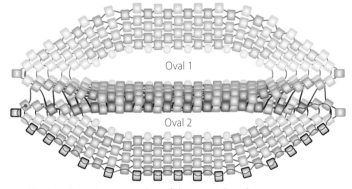

Add A beads to the outer edge of the second oval.

figure 8

Join the third, fourth, and fifth pointed ovals as described above. Weave in the thread and clip after joining each oval to the previous one, except the last one. Before joining the inner edges of the sixth and first ovals, insert the resin bead.

Note: It isn't necessary to add inner edge D beads or outer edge A beads to the sixth oval because they're already in place on the first and fifth ovals.

Join the points of the pointed ovals at each end with a C bead between each point. Weave in the thread and clip.

Add Crystals

Anchor a new doubled thread at the top of the bauble. Stitch in the ditch along the beads in row 5 of each oval with D. Then pass along the edge of each oval adding a 2.5-mm bicone crystal between D beads.

At the bottom end of the bauble, add a fringe or picot between the point beads, if you wish.

Leaves—First Layer

The leaves are small pointed ovals made with two layers following the directions for the Basic Pointed Oval on page 116. Vary the A, B, and C beads in these leaves in any way you like. Attach the leaves between the point beads at the top of the bauble. Make six two-layer leaves.

With 2 yards (about 2 m) of thread in the needle, bring the ends together, wax well, knot, clip the tail close to the knot, and melt the ends slightly.

Row 1: String 1 A, 5 Bs, 4 As, 5 Bs, and 3 As.

	Corners	Sides
Row 2:	2 As	4 Bs
Row 3:	2 As	5 Bs
Row 4:	1 A	6 Bs

To stitch the second layer, weave through A beads to the first layer's starting row as shown in the Basic Pointed Oval on page 116.

	Corners	Sides
Row 1:	2 As	3 Bs
Row 2:	2 As	4 Bs
Row 3:	2 As	5 Bs

Zip the second layer to the first along the outer edge. At the corners, pass through the first A on the second layer, the single bead at the tip of the first layer, and the next A on the second layer. Weave in the thread and clip.

Assemble

String a bead cap and an 8-mm round crystal onto the head pin. Insert the head pin through the bottom of the beadwork and resin bead. String the 6-mm bicone crystal and the second bead cap onto the head pin.

Using round-nose pliers, make a loop with the tail end of the head pin close to the bead cap and attach the bail to the loop. Close the loop and trim the excess wire.

Variation

Beaded by Dana Steen Witker and Rita Linton

SUPPLIES

Size 11° cylinder beads:

A (shown in brown), 15 g

Size 15° seed beads:

B (shown in yellow), 1 g

8 emerald green 32 x 17-mm navette stones with foil back (Swarovski 4227)

18 bronze 4-mm round beads

Two-strand clasp

Metallic foiled leather, 7 x 1½ inches (18 x 3.8 cm)

Glue (E6000 or Goop)

FireLine 6 lb

Size 10 beading needle

Microcrystalline wax

Scissors

Lighter

DIMENSIONS

8 inches (20.5 cm)

NAVETTE BRACELET

Pointed ovals take on a new role as bezels for navette stones. This popular shape never goes out of style. To make the finished length absolutely perfect, adjust the total number of navettes in your bracelet or the number of round beads used to connect them.

Prepare the Navette Stones

Glue a piece of foiled leather to the backs of the navette stones to prevent scratches. Trace around the stone and cut the leather to fit. Put a small dab of glue in the center back of the leather and hold it against the stone for a few minutes until the glue has set. Trim the excess leather from around the edge of the stone. Set aside to dry.

The pointed oval bezel is made in two layers, a front and a back. After making the front layer, zip it to the back layer around the outer edge. Insert the stone when you're halfway around.

Pointed Oval Bezel—Front Layer

With 2 yards (about 2 m) of thread in your needle, bring the ends together, wax well, knot, clip the tail close to the knot, and melt the ends slightly.

Make the front layer as for the Basic Pointed Oval on page 116.

Row 1: String 54 As.

	Corners	Sides
Row 2:	2 As	13 As
Row 3:	2 As	14 As
Row 4:	1 A	15 As

Stitch the Inner Ring

Pass through the column of beads at the end of the pointed oval so the thread exits the first "down" bead (closest to the center) of the inner ring. Peyote around with B, adding 1 B in the valley formed at each point for a total of 26 Bs. Weave in the thread and clip (**figure 1**).

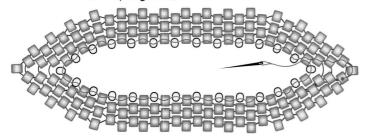

figure 1

Pointed Oval Bezel—Back Layer

Row 1: String 46 As.

	Corners	Sides
Row 2:	2 As	11 As
Row 3:	2 As	12 As
Row 4:	2 As	13 As
Row 5:	2 As	14 As

Join the Layers

Align the front and back layers and zip them together halfway around along the outer edge. Insert the leather-backed stone and continue zipping. Weave in the thread and clip.

Repeat these steps to add a bezel to the remaining navette stones.

Join the Navettes

Start a new thread along the edge of one bezel. Working along the zipped row, exit through the sixth bead. Add a round bead and pass through the corresponding bead on a second bezel. Pass back through the round bead and the bead at the start of this step on the first bezel. Repeat to reinforce the connection.

Weave through beads along the zipped edge on the first bezel, exit through the sixth bead from the opposite tip, and make a second connection as above (**figure 2**).

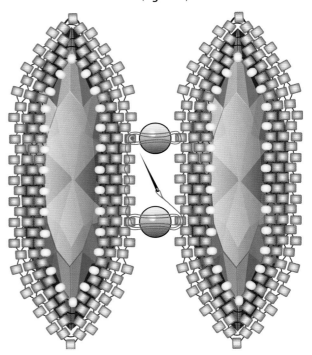

figure 2

Make one more pass through the round bead and exit the connecting bead on the second bezel.

Weave through the beads on the back of the second bezel and exit through the sixth bead on the zipped row as before. Continue until you've connected the eighth navette to the seventh. Weave through the back of the bezel on the eighth navette.

Add the Clasp

Repeat the round bead connection as described above, but attach each round bead on the outer edge of the eighth navette to one clasp loop. Make several passes with the thread to reinforce the connection. Weave in the thread and clip. Repeat on the outer edge of the first navette, making sure the clasp is correctly positioned when the bracelet is closed.

Navette Pendant

SUPPLIES

Size 11° cylinder beads:

   A (silver), 3 g

Size 15° seed beads:

   B (silver) < 1 g

1 silver 32 x 17-mm navette stone with foil back (Swarovski 4227)

33 silver 1.8-mm cube beads

1 soldered jump ring, 6 mm

Metallic foiled leather, 1½ inches (3.8 cm) square

Glue (E6000 or Goop)

FireLine 6 lb

Size 10 beading needle

Microcrystalline wax

Scissors

Lighter

DIMENSIONS

1½ x 1 inch (3.8 x 1.5 cm)

A single navette stone makes a striking pendant. Follow the directions for the navette bezel on page 131, stitching cube beads along the zipped edge, including the bottom point on the bezel. Then, instead of adding a cube bead at the top point, stitch on a soldered jump ring to use as your bail. Hang it from a favorite chain.

SUPPLIES

Size 11° cylinder beads:

  A (shown in brown), 8 g

  B (shown in yellow), 7 g

  C (shown in green), 4 g

Size 15° Japanese seed beads:

  D (shown in orange), 2 g

10 blue 8-mm round crystals (Swarovski 5000)

320 blue 3-mm bicone crystals (Swarovski 5328)

11 bronze 4-mm flattened bicone beads

2 bronze 3-mm round beads

1 lobster-claw clasp with 6-mm jump ring

FireLine 6 lb

Size 10 beading needle

Microcrystalline wax

Scissors

Lighter

DIMENSIONS

20 inches (51 cm)

EYE OF APOLLO NECKLACE

This project features 10 embellished ovals stitched end to end.

Work the pointed ovals for this necklace following the directions for the Basic Pointed Oval on page 116, with these changes:

Row 1: String 1 A, 19 Cs, 4 As, 19 Cs, and 3 As.

	Corners	Sides
Row 2:	2 As	11 Bs
Row 3:	2 As	12 Bs
Row 4:	2 As	13 Bs
Row 5:	2 As	14 As
Row 6:	1 A	15 As

Add the Round Crystal

Add the round crystal before starting the second layer, as for the Pirate Eyes Bracelet on page 119. Work the second layer off the starting row as on page 119, continuing the colors and bead counts indicated on rows 2–5 of this chart. Zip the outer edges together.

Repeat all steps to make a total of 10 pointed ovals.

Add Fringe

Thread 2 yards (about 2 m) of thread, bring the ends together, wax well, knot, clip the tail close to the knot, and melt the ends slightly. Exit an A bead in row 5 of the first layer.

Add one bicone crystal and 1 D. Pass back through the crystal and pass through the next A on row 6. Repeat around the oval. At the points, pass through the single A and add a bicone crystal and 1 D. Pass through the A again in the same direction.

Join the Pointed Ovals

Anchor a doubled thread in a pointed oval and exit an A at one tip. String a 4-mm flattened bicone, pass through the A at the tip of a second pointed oval, then pass back through the bicone. Go back and forth through the bicone to reinforce the connection, keeping the pointed ovals flat and the threads parallel (**figure 1**). (If the threads cross in the bicone, the finished necklace may twist.) Weave through beads and repeat this step to join all 10 pointed ovals.

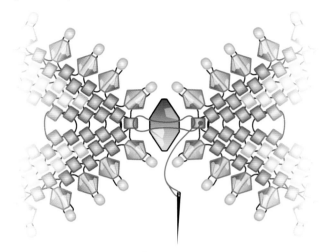

figure 1

Add the Clasp

With your thread exiting the A at the tip of the 10th oval, add one 4-mm flattened bicone and one 3-mm round bead and pass through the loop on the clasp. Pass back through the two beads just added and the A at the tip of the oval. Repeat to reinforce the connection, weave in the thread, and clip. Attach the jump ring to the other end of the necklace the same way.

Note: To make the necklace longer, stitch additional ovals or use a short length of chain in place of the jump ring.

SUPPLIES

Size 11° cylinder beads:

A (outer edge and corners), 4 g

B (main color), 4 g

C (inner edge color), 2 g

Size 15° Japanese seed beads:

D (embellishment), 1 g

4 blue 8-mm round crystals (Swarovski 5000)

128 blue 3-mm bicone crystals (Swarovski 5328)

8 inches (20.3 cm) of 20-gauge brass wire

1 pin back, 1½ inches (4 cm) long

FireLine 6 lb

Size 10 beading needle

Microcrystalline wax

Scissors

Lighter

DIMENSIONS

3½ inches (9 cm) wide

Wings

Make four pointed ovals following the directions for the ovals in the Eye of Apollo Necklace on page 134.

Body

Make one pointed oval for the body as follows:

First Layer

Row 1: String 1 A, 9 Cs, 4 As, 9 Cs, and 3 As.

	Corners	Sides
Row 2:	2 As	6 Bs
Row 3:	2 As	7 Bs
Row 4:	1 A	8 Bs

Second Layer

Row 1:	2 As	6 Bs
Row 2:	2 As	7 Bs

Zip the outer edges together.

Sew the lower wings so they overlap the top wings. Center the body over the joined wings and stitch it into place. Form the antennae out of a single piece of wire, cut off the excess, and sew at the bend to the back of the body. Stitch the pin back to the butterfly at a point just above the center back.

Chapter 7
POTPOURRI

Just for fun, take the basic shapes in myriad new directions ranging from whimsical to geometric.

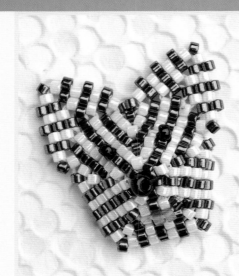

FINGERS IN MY POCKET DOLL

Arms akimbo and fingers in her pockets, this doll's stance says she's confident and ready for anything. With sneakers, striped-and-ruffled socks, bracelets, necklace, and tiny hat, she's as pert and sassy as you make her. Wear her as a pendant, add a pin back to wear her as a brooch, or simply keep her nearby when you need someone to talk to.

Making the basic doll is easy. She has an elongated triangle body, straight tube legs, and angled arms—all worked in peyote stitch. It's important to work with soft tension throughout so her parts can be easily sewn together.

SUPPLIES

Size 11° cylinder beads:

  A (shown in dark gray), 6 g

  B (shown in pink), 3 g

Size 15° seed beads:

  C (shown in light gray), 1 g

2 black 15 x 9-mm Czech pressed-glass tennis shoe beads

One 4-mm closed jump ring, 3-mm bead, or size 8° seed bead

1 bead cap (for hat)

1 wood 14–15-mm bead*

Miscellaneous small beads for the doll's bracelet and necklace

Tiny buttons for the dress front (optional)

5 inches (12 cm) of 22-gauge wire

White glue

Clear nail polish*

Fine-point permanent markers*

Nymo D or FireLine 6 lb

Size 10 beading needle

Microcrystalline wax

Scissors

Lighter

Wire cutters

Round-nose pliers

*** Instead, you can omit this item and use a porcelain face bead.**

DIMENSIONS

3½ x 2 inches (9 x 5 cm)

Arm—First Layer

With 2 yards (about 2 m) of thread in your needle, bring the ends together, and wax well.

Row 1: String a stopper bead and 24 As (**figure 1**).

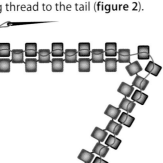

figure 1

Row 2: Peyote 6 with A. Add 2 As, skip one bead in the row below, and pass through the next A. Peyote 5 with A. Remove the stopper bead and tie the working thread to the tail (**figure 2**).

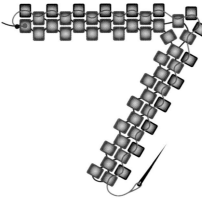

figure 2

Row 3: Peyote 6 with A, exiting the first A of the pair of A in row 2. Add 2 As and pass through the second A. Peyote 6 with A (**figure 3**).

Row 4: Peyote 7 with A, exiting the first A of the pair of A in row 3. Add 2 As and pass through the second A. Peyote 6 with A (**figure 4**).

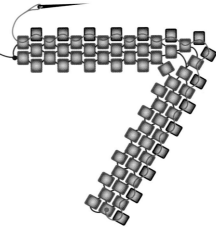

figure 4

Row 5: Peyote 7 with A, exiting the first A of the pair of A in row 4. Add 2 As and pass through the second A. Peyote 7 with A (**figure 5**).

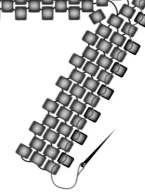

figure 5

Row 6: Peyote 8 with A, exiting the first bead of the pair of A in row 5. Add 1 A and pass through the second A. Peyote 7 with A (**figure 6**).

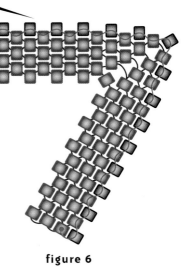

figure 6

Weave through edge beads and exit the first bead of the first row, pointing away from the work (**figure 7**).

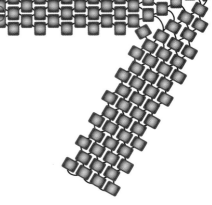

figure 7

Arm—Second Layer

Row 1: Peyote 12 with A.

Row 2: Peyote 6 with A. Add 2 As, skip one A, and pass through the next A. Peyote 5 with A.

Row 3: Peyote 6 with A, exiting the first A of the pair of A in row 2. Add 2 As and pass through the second A. Peyote 6 with A.

Row 4: Peyote 7 with A, exiting the first A of the pair of A in row 3. Add 2 As and pass through the second A. Peyote 6 with A.

Row 5: Peyote 7 with A, exiting the first A of the pair of A in row 4. Add 2 As and pass through the second A. Peyote 7 with A.

Zip the outer edge of the first layer to the outer edge of the second layer. Weave in the thread and clip. Repeat these steps to make a second arm.

Legs with Striped Socks

With 2 yards (about 2 m) of thread in your needle, bring the ends together and wax well.

Row 1: String a stopper bead. String 2 As and 2 Bs five times, then add 2 As for a total of 22 beads (**figure 8**).

figure 8

Rows 2–11: Peyote 11 across each row, adding As above the As and Bs above the Bs. Remove the stopper bead and tie the working thread to the tail after row 2 (**figure 9**).

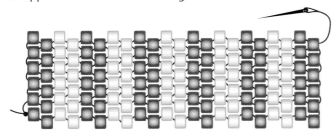

figure 9

Zip the last row to the first to form a tube. Sew a shoe bead to the bottom of the tube. Weave in the thread and clip. Repeat these steps to make a second leg.

Leg Ruffles

Making these is optional.

Row 1: String 14 Cs. Before closing the ring, place the beads around the top of the shoe.

Row 2: Add 3 Cs, skip the next bead in the ring, and pass through the second bead. Repeat around the ring. Weave in the thread and clip.

Repeat to make a ruffle around the second leg.

Body—Back Layer

Use B for the skirt and A for the rest of the body.

With 2½ yards (about 2.5 m) of thread in your needle, bring the ends together and wax well, knot, clip the tail close to the knot, and melt the ends slightly.

Row 1: String 2 As and 1 B and form a ring secured with a lark's head knot as follows: Push the beads to within 1 inch (2.5 cm) of the knot. Separate the strands between

the beads and the knot. Pass the needle between the strands, tighten, then pass back through the last bead strung (**figures 10** and **11**). Don't allow the knot to slip into a bead. Orient the work so you're working counterclockwise (lefties, work clockwise).

figure 10

figure 11

Row 2: *Add 1 B and 1 A and pass through the next A on the ring. Add 4 As and pass through the next A. Add 1 A and 1 B and pass through the next B. Step up. Make sure the beads at each corner are almost parallel. Adjust them if necessary (**figure 12**).

figure 12

Variation

Variations

Note: For this triangle, the step up is always at the same corner.

Row 3: Add 1 B and 1 A and pass through the next A.

• Add 1 A and pass through the next 2 As.

• Add 4 As and pass through the next 2 As.

• Add 1 A and pass through the next A.

• Add 1 A and 1 B and pass through the next B.

• Add 1 B and pass through the next B. Step up (**figure 13**).

figure 13

Row 4: Add 1 B and 1 A and pass through the next A.

• Add 1 A and pass through the next A.

• Add 2 As and pass through the next 2 As.

• Add 4 As and pass through the next 2 As.

• Add 2 As and pass through the next A.

• Add 1 A and pass through the next A.

• Add 1 A and 1 B and pass through the next B.

• Peyote twice with B. Step up (**figure 14**).

figure 14

Rows 5–10: Work as for row 4, adding 1 B and 1 A at the right corner, 4 As at the upper corner, and 1 A and 1 B at the left corner. Peyote the sides with A, adding 1 A above each single A and 2 As above each pair of As. Peyote across the bottom with B. Leave the thread attached.

Body—Front Layer

Work the body's front layer following the directions for the back layer, but with this change: Stitch one more row, row 11, using a single A at the two bottom corners. Don't add beads at the top point. Continue the peyote pattern on the sides. Weave in the thread and clip.

Assemble

Sew the arms and legs to the body's back layer as shown in **figure 15**.

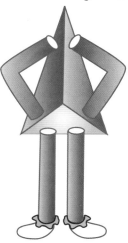

figure 15

To attach the head, fold the wire in half and slide a closed jump ring or 3-mm bead to the center. Insert the wire ends through the bead cap. Wrap the next ½ inch (1.3 cm) of wire with thread so it fits securely inside the head bead. Test this to make sure you have a tight fit, then remove it. Trim the ends of the wire as needed.

Saturate the thread with glue and reinsert it into the head. Add more glue inside the bead hole and allow to dry. The jump ring or 3-mm bead is now at the top, and the optional bead cap fits over the face bead like a hat.

Use round-nose pliers to bend circles in the ends of the wire. Sew the wire to the inside of the body's back layer (**figure 16**).

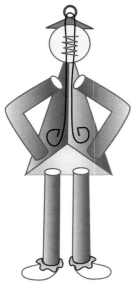

figure 16

Zip the body's front and back sections together, stitching through the arms and legs as necessary to continue the zipping pattern. Weave in the thread and clip.

If you're using a wood bead instead of a porcelain face bead, you'll need to paint a face on it. First, coat the bead with nail polish, then add features with a fine-point permanent marker. Use black for eyes and hair, and red for lips (**figure 17**).

figure 17

Embellish the doll as you'd like, adding a necklace, bracelets, and decorative buttons sewn to the front of her dress.

Cat Doll

You'll need all the supplies listed for the Fingers in My Pocket Doll except for the head, plus the ones below.

SUPPLIES

4 inches (10 cm) of black 18-gauge wire

15 inches (38 cm) of black 24-gauge wire

6 inches (15 cm) of ribbon, ½ inch (1.3 cm) wide

DIMENSIONS

4 x 2 inches (10.2 x 5.1 cm)

Head

Follow the directions on page 152 to make the cat's head. When zipping the back and front of the head together, leave the bottom edge open. Insert the top of the body triangle and sew the cat's head to the body.

Arms, Legs, and Body

Follow the directions on page 138 for the doll's arms, legs, and body, changing the patterns and colors as you like.

Tail

Wrap the piece of 18-gauge wire with the 24-gauge wire in a spiral 3 inches (7.5 cm) long. Make a tiny loop with round-nose pliers at one end of the heavier wire. Insert the other end of the heavier wire through the beginning ring of the back triangle so that the wire passes through to the wrong side. Form a loop on the wrong side of the back triangle and sew this loop securely in place. Form the tail into a curve as shown and trim or file any rough ends.

Add a ribbon bow around the cat's neck. Stitch a pin back to the body's back layer or sew a jump ring to the cat's head to use as a pendant bail.

Size 11° cylinder beads:

  A (main color, shown in brown), 10 g

  B (dark purple for eye liner), < 1 g

  C (silver-lined blue accent), < 1 g

  D (matte gold accent), < 1 g

1 Kemper oval 18-mm doll eye with a flat back

8 crystal AB 5-mm rose montees

7 amethyst 7-mm rose montees

6 emerald 4-mm rose montees

5 light amethyst 5-mm rose montees

2¼ x 1½-inch (5.5 x 3.8 cm) piece of felt

FireLine 6 lb

Size 10 beading needle

Microcrystalline wax

Scissors

Lighter

DIMENSIONS

2 x 3 inches (5 x 7.5 cm)

EYE OF PROVIDENCE PENDANT

The Eye of Providence, sometimes referred to as the all-seeing eye, appears on the dollar bill but it dates back to ancient Egyptian mythology, representing God watching over mankind. The eye symbol, sometimes shown with rays emanating from it, may also be surrounded by a triangle.

This striking pendant consists of two elongated triangles sewn together with a pointed oval bezel framing the glass doll eye. For embellishment, use rose montees and nail heads as shown here. Or, try embellishing with other decorative items, including roses, as shown on page 145.

Triangle—Front Layer

Rows 1–4: Using A beads only, follow the instructions for rows 1–4 of the Fingers in My Pocket Doll body on page 139.

Rows 5–18: Continue for another 14 rows, adding 2 As at the left and right corners and 4 As at the lower corner. Peyote the sides with A, adding 1 A above each single A and 2 As above each pair of As.

Row 19: Work as for row 18, but add only 1 A at the left and right corners and 3 As at the upper corner. When you complete this row, you'll have 17 "up" beads across the bottom of the triangle, not counting the single corner beads. Don't step up through the single bead at the end of row 19. The lower edge now becomes the top of the triangle.

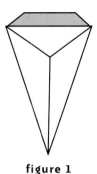

figure 1

Triangle—Extension

This extension, shown in gray in **figure 1**, forms the front of a channel for the necklace chain. To make it, begin with the thread exiting the last bead on row 19. Turn and pass back through the last bead just added. Peyote across the row, adding 17 As to the top of the triangle (**figure 2**).

figure 2

Work 10 more rows. At the end of each row, turn and pass back through the last bead added, then work back across the row in peyote stitch with A.

Work back and forth with decreases at both ends of each row until there are seven "up" beads remaining across the row. Weave in the thread and clip (**figure 3**).

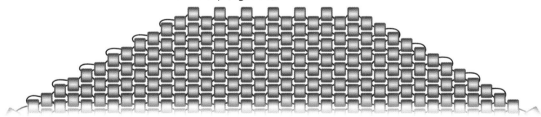

figure 3

Pointed Oval Eye Bezel

Row 1: String 3 As, 15 Bs, 4 As, 15 Bs, and 1 A and form a ring secured with a lark's head knot as follows: Push the beads to within 1 inch (2.5 cm) of the knot. Separate the strands between the beads and the knot. Pass the needle between the strands, tighten, then pass back through the last bead strung (**figure 4**). Don't allow the knot to slip into a bead. Orient the beads so you're working counterclockwise (lefties, work clockwise). Keep the piece flat as you work.

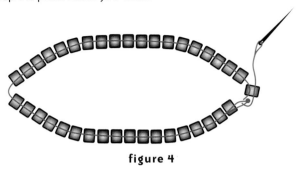

figure 4

Row 2: *Add 2 As and pass through the next A. Don't skip a bead. Peyote 9 with A. Repeat from * once. Step up (**figure 5**).

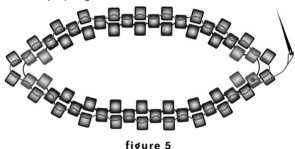

figure 5

Rows 3–6: Repeat row 2 four times. Each row will have one more bead on the top half and on the bottom half. Step up at the end of each row.

Row 7: Peyote around with A. Add only 1 A between the pairs of A at each point. You'll have seven pairs of A and a single A at each corner (**figure 6**).

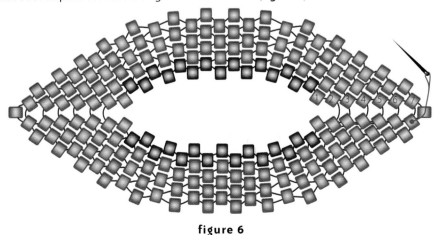

figure 6

Sew the oval bezel to the pendant front, positioning the bezel's center just above the beginning ring of the triangle (**figure 7**). Before completely attaching the bezel, slip the glass eye into place, then complete the stitching.

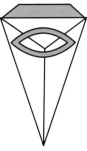

figure 7

Note: When sewing two pieces of bead-work together, treat them like pieces of fabric, poking the needle down between beads and coming back up between beads. If you prefer that the thread not show on the back, then pass through beads to the next point where you want a stitch.

Embellish the Bezel

Sew the 5-mm crystal AB rose montees in a curved line along the bezel's top edge. Sew the 7-mm amethyst rose montees above the crystal AB rose montees, following the upper edge of the triangle extension.

Working along the bezel's lower edge, backstitch a single row of beads with C (**figure 8**). Backstitch a single row with D below the row of Cs.

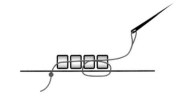

Backstitch: *With your thread exiting the front of the work, string four beads. Pass through the piece and come back up between the second and third beads. Pass forward through the third and fourth beads.*

figure 8

Following the curved line of back-stitched beads below the bezel, sew on the six 4-mm emerald rose montees. Sew on the five 5-mm light amethyst rose montees below these. Weave in the thread and clip.

Triangle—Back Layer and Extension

Work rows 1–18 as for the front layer. (Don't add row 19.) You'll have 16 "up" beads across the top of the triangle, not counting the corner beads. At the end of row 18, don't step up.

Add 1 A, turn, and pass back through the next A. Work back and forth across the top as for the front layer until there are eight "up" beads.

Assemble

Zip the last row of the back extension to the last row of the front extension, leaving the diagonal side edges open.

Pass through edge beads to exit the single bead at the left or right corner of row 19 of the front triangle. To make the triangle stiff and slightly rounded, place two layers of felt inside. Photocopy **figure 9**, cut it out, and use it as a template to cut out a piece of felt. Cut a second piece ⅛ inch (3 mm) smaller on all sides. Glue or stitch the two layers together.

Place the two layers of felt between the back and front triangle.

Zip the front triangle to the back triangle along the two long edges of the triangle. Weave in the thread and clip. To wear, insert a chain through the channel at the top of the pendant.

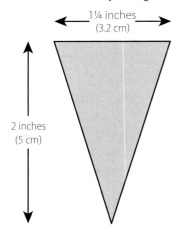

1¼ inches
(3.2 cm)

2 inches
(5 cm)

figure 9

Eye of Providence with Roses

SUPPLIES

Size 11° cylinder beads:

A (shown in rust), 3 g

B (shown in yellow), 3 g

Size 11° seed beads:

C (shown in dark gray), 10 g

5 topaz 3-mm bicone crystals
(Swarovski 5328)

1 bronze 3-mm faceted round bead

45 jet 2-mm round crystals
(Swarovski 5000)

750 jet 3-mm bicone crystals
(Swarovski 5328)

14-mm closed ring

2 fold-over end covers

Lobster-claw clasp with 6-mm
jump ring

2 jump rings, 4 mm

20 inches (51 cm) of 2-mm cotton cord

FireLine 6 lb

Size 10 beading needle

Microcrystalline wax

Scissors

Lighter

Flat-nose pliers

DIMENSIONS

Starfish: 1½ inches (3.8 cm)

Necklace: 19 inches (48.5 cm)

STARFISH NECKLACE

Starfish are radially symmetric undersea creatures that exist in a wide variety of colors. This is a fun project to make!

Starfish Points

With 2 yards (about 2 m) of thread in your needle, bring the ends together, wax well, knot, clip the tail close to the knot, and melt the ends slightly.

Note: Work with soft tension to keep the bottom flat.

Row 1: String 5 As and form a ring secured with a lark's head knot as follows: Push the beads to within 1 inch (2.5 cm) of the knot. Separate the strands between the beads and the knot. Pass the needle between the strands, tighten, then pass back through the last bead strung (**figures 1** and **2**). Don't allow the knot to slip into a bead. Orient the work so you're working counterclockwise (lefties, work clockwise).

figure 1

figure 2

Row 2: *Add 1 B and pass through the next bead. Don't skip a bead. Repeat from * four more times. Step up (**figure 3**).

figure 3

Row 3: *Add 2 As and pass through the next B. Repeat from * four more times. Step up through 1 A (**figure 4**). The A beads form the corners of the base pentagon.

figure 4

Row 4: *Add 1 A and pass through the next A at this corner. Add 1 B and pass through the first A at the next corner. Repeat from * four more times. Step up (**figure 5**).

figure 5

Row 5: Peyote around with B. Step up (**figure 6**).

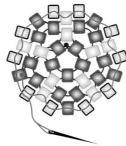

figure 6

Row 6: *Peyote once with B. Add 3 As and pass through the next B. Repeat from * four more times. Step up (**figure 7**).

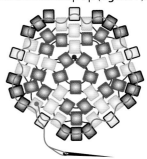

figure 7

Note: The center A in each 3 A set needs to be indented. Push it into place with your fingernail if necessary.

Row 7: Peyote once with B. *Add 2 As and pass through the third A of this set of 3 As. Peyote twice with B. Repeat from * four more times, but on the last repeat, peyote only once. Step up (**figure 8**).

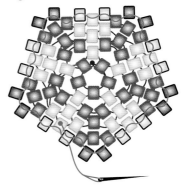

figure 8

Row 8: Peyote once with B. *Add 1 A and pass through the next A. Peyote 3 with B. Repeat from * four more times, but on the last repeat, peyote twice with B instead of three times. Step up (**figure 9**).

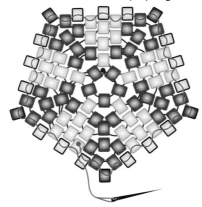

figure 9

Row 9: Peyote around with B. Step up (**figure 10**).

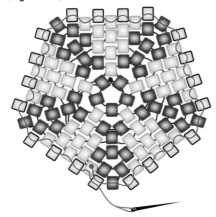

figure 10

Mid-Side Increases

Row 10: *Keeping the tension soft, add 3 As at this corner and pass through the next B. Peyote once with B. Add 2 As and pass through the next "up" B. Peyote once with B. Repeat from * four more times. Step up (**figure 11**).

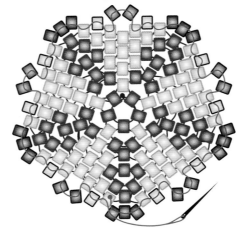

figure 11

Rows 11–19: Refer to the chart in the next column. Use A at the corners and for the mid-side increases. Use B between the corners and the mid-side increases.

Note: The number of peyote stitches between the corner and the mid-side increase will increase by one on each side of the increase on almost every row. Don't miss adding a B before and after the increase!

Row	Corners	Between Corner and Mid-Side Increase	Mid-Side Increase
11	2 As	2 Bs	2 As
12	1 A	3 Bs	2 As
13	0	4 Bs	2 As
14	3 As	4 Bs	2 As
15	2 As	5 Bs	2 As
16	1 A	6 Bs	2 As
17	0	7 Bs	2 As
18	3 As	7 Bs	2 As
19	2 As	8 Bs	2 As

Join the Edges

Pass through beads so the thread exits the A at the inner tip of the next mid-side increase. Add 1 A and pass through the next A at this increase.

Peyote 9 with C along this edge and exit the first bead of the pair of C on the outer tip of the point. Add one 3-mm bicone and 1 A. Pass back through the bicone and the next A on the opposite side at this corner.

Zip the edge just completed to the other side of this point, working toward the center. Pass through the Cs just added on one side and the As on the other side.

Repeat this step for the remaining four points, with this exception: To form a bail, on the last point, instead of adding a single A after the 3-mm bicone, add 10 As. Pass the As through the closed 14-mm ring, pass back through the 3-mm bicone, and finish zipping the point.

Pass through the five beads in the center to close the hole. Sew the 3-mm faceted round bead in the center.

Embellish

Using doubled thread as before, anchor the thread at the outer tip of a point. Add a line of nine 2-mm crystals along the top of each point, stitching in the ditch and passing through the As that join the two sides of the arm.

Netted Tube with Crystals

The netted tube is worked around the cotton cord. Place one end of the cord in a fold-over end cover and, using pliers, squeeze each side of the end cover over the cord. With 3 yards (about 3 m) of thread in your needle, bring the ends together, wax well, knot, clip the tail close to the knot, and melt the ends slightly.

String 6 Cs and form a ring secured with a lark's head knot as before. Pass back through the last bead added (**figure 12**). Insert the cord into the ring of beads and tighten the ring. Pass through the cord just below the fold-over end cover (**figure 13**). Work clockwise while stitching the netting (lefties, work counterclockwise).

figure 12

figure 13

*Add one 3-mm bicone crystal and 2 Cs. Pass through the second C from where your thread is exiting (**figure 14**). Repeat from * one more time (**figure 15**).

figure 14

figure 15

Add one 3-mm bicone crystal and 2 Cs. Pass through the first C after the next bicone. Repeat from * for the desired length (**figure 16**). Place the remaining end of the cord in a fold-over end cover and, using pliers, squeeze each side of the end cover over the cord.

figure 16

Finish

Add 1 C and pass through the first C after the next bicone three times. Pull tight. Pass through the cord just below the end cover and the three Cs again. Knot between the beads twice, pass through several beads, and clip the tails.

Attach a 4-mm jump ring to each end cover. Attach the lobster claw clasp to one jump ring and the 6-mm jump ring to the other. For an adjustable-length necklace, add a short piece of chain in place of the 6-mm jump ring.

Did Darwin miss this species?

SUE CLARK
Psychedelic Starfish March to the Sea!
Photo by artist

SUPPLIES

Size 11° cylinder beads:

A (shown in black), 8 g

B (shown in silver), 3 g

C (shown in red), 3 g

1 black 3-mm faceted round bead

1 pin back (with or without bail),
1¼ inches (3.2 cm) long

Nymo D or FireLine 6 lb

Size 10 beading needle

Microcrystalline wax

Scissors

Lighter

DIMENSIONS

2¾ inches (7 cm) in diameter

Variations

Beaded by Carmian Seifert (top)
and Sonya Monzel (bottom)

STACKED PENTAGON PIN OR PENDANT

This three-dimensional pin or pendant has two layers: the front layer is stacked; the back layer is flat. Connect the front, which is offset from the back, to the back's last row. With its strong geometric shape, it has the appeal of Art Deco jewelry. Made with other colors than shown here, it takes on an entirely different look.

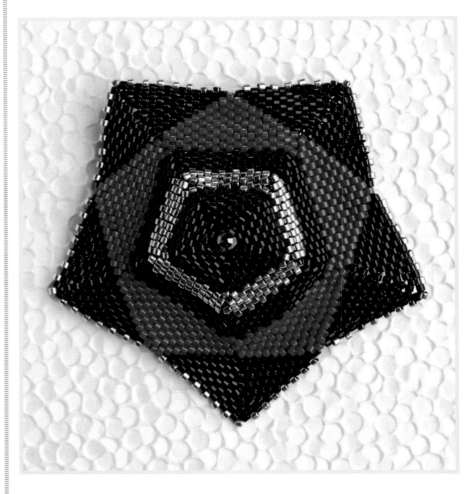

Front Layer—Pentagon

Rows 1–9: Follow the directions for rows 1–9 of the Starfish Necklace on page 147, but work with all A beads.

Rows 10–26: Follow the chart on page 151 for the number of beads to increase at each corner, the number of beads to peyote on each side, and the color. On the rows with zero at the corner, don't add beads—simply pass through the single bead on the previous row.

Front Layer

Row	Corners	Sides	Color
10*	1	3	A
11*	0	4	A
12	3	3	B
13	2	4	B
14	1	5	B
15	0	6	B
16*	1	5	B
17*	0	6	B
18	3	5	A
19	2	6	A
20	1	7	A
21	0	8	A
22*	1	7	A
23*	0	8	A
24	3	7	C
25	2	8	C
26	1	9	C

* Indicates tubular peyote without increases at the corners. When there are increases, you're stitching a flat, circular plane with a widening diameter. The rows with * don't enlarge the diameter; they help form the sides of the stepped shape (**figure 1**).

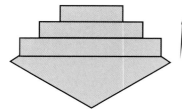

figure 1

Front Layer—Points

Create the points on each side of the pentagon by decreasing at the beginning and end of each of the next rows.

Rows 27–36: Pass through beads so the thread is exiting a single C at the corner. Peyote 10 with C. After exiting the single C at the next corner, turn, and without adding a bead, pass back through the last C added. Work back and forth across these rows in peyote stitch until one bead remains in the row (**figure 2**).

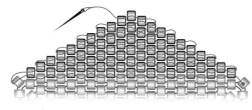

figure 2

Pass back through the single bead, then pass through all the beads along the left diagonal edge (**figure 3**).

figure 3

Repeat this step to add points to the remaining four sides of the pentagon. Sew the 3-mm bead to the center front.

Back Layer

Rows 1–9: Follow the directions for rows 1–9 of the Starfish Necklace on page 147, but work with all A beads.

Follow the chart in the next colum to stitch a flat pentagon for the back layer. Use A beads for all rows except the last. Don't trim the thread.

Back Layer

Row	Corners	Sides	Color
10	3	3	A
11	2	4	A
12	1	5	A
13	0	6	A
14	3	5	A
15	2	6	A
16	1	7	A
17	0	8	A
18	3	7	A
19	2	8	A
20	1	9	A
21	0	10	A
22	3	9	A
23	2	10	A
24	1	11	A
25	0	12	A
26	3	11	A
27	2	12	A
28	1	13	A
29	0	14	A
30	3	13	A
31	2	14	A

Add the Pin Back

Start a new thread and sew the pin back in place about ½ inch (1.3 cm) below the edge, centering it between two points on the back layer. If you're using a pin back with a bail, keep the bail centered and right below the back layer's edge and out of sight.

Join the Front and Back Layers

The front and back are connected only at the corners of the front. Continuing with the thread from row 31 of the back, weave through beads to exit the A before a point. *Add 1 B (the single B between the pair of As at the point), then peyote 7 with B. To attach the front layer, pass through the single C on one of the front layer's points. Peyote 7 with B as before. Repeat from * four more times. Weave in the thread and trim.

SUPPLIES

Size 11° cylinder beads:

A (shown in light gray), 3 g

B (shown in brown), 3 g

2 black 3-mm round nail heads (for eyes) or size 11° seed beads

1 black 3-mm round bead (for the nose) or size 8° seed bead

1 red 3-mm nail head (for the mouth) or size 8° seed bead

Nymo D or FireLine 6 lb

Size 10 beading needle

Microcrystalline wax

Scissors

Lighter

DIMENSIONS

1 x 1 inch (2.5 x 2.5 cm)

CUTE CAT (OR DOG) FACE

Who can resist the mug of a cute little kitty or pooch? This beadwork is a pentagon made with cylinder beads in two colors, using the hexagon and triangle increase patterns. Use it as a bead, pin, pendant, or charm.

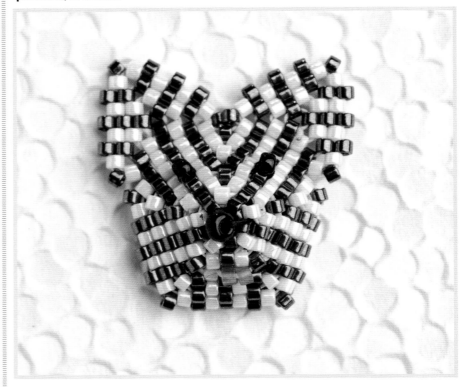

With 2 yards (about 2 m) of thread in your needle, bring the ends together, wax well, knot, clip the tail close to the knot, and melt the ends slightly.

Front Layer—Face

Row 1: String 5 Bs and form a ring secured with a lark's head knot as follows: Push the beads to within 1 inch (2.5 cm) of the knot. Separate the strands between the beads and the knot. Pass the needle between the strands, tighten, then pass back through the last bead strung (**figures 1** and **2**). Don't allow the knot to slip into a bead. Orient the work so you're working counterclockwise (lefties, work clockwise).

figure 1

figure 2

Row 2: *Add 1 A and pass through the next B. Don't skip a bead. Repeat from * four more times. Step up (**figure 3**).

figure 3

Row 3: *Add 1 B and pass through the next A. Repeat from * four more times. Step up (**figure 4**).

figure 4

Row 4: *Add 2 As and pass through the next B. Repeat from * four more times. Step up (**figure 5**).

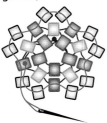

figure 5

Row 5: *Add 1 B between the two As at the corner. Peyote once with B. Repeat from * four more times. Step up (**figure 6**).

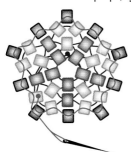

figure 6

Row 6: Peyote around with A. Step up (**figure 7**).

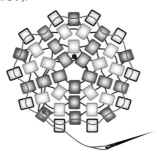

figure 7

Row 7: *Peyote once with B. Add 2 Bs at the corner. Repeat from * four more times. Step up (**figure 8**).

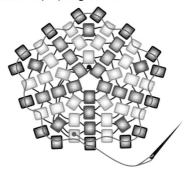

figure 8

Row 8: Peyote once with A*. Add 1 A between the 2 Bs at the corner. Peyote

twice with A. Repeat from * four more times. Peyote once with A. Step up (**figure 9**).

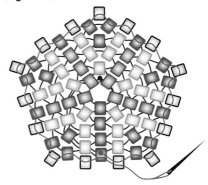

figure 9

Row 9: Peyote around with B. Step up (**figure 10**).

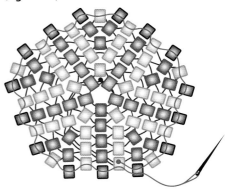

figure 10

Variations

Beaded by Ann Gilbert (top left), Carmian Seifert (top right), and Jane Langenback (bottom row)

Row 10: *Add 2 As and pass through the next B. Peyote twice with A. Repeat from * four more times. Step up (**figure 11**).

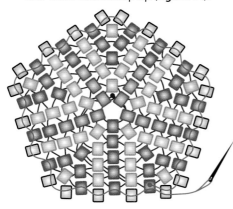

figure 11

Row 11: *Add 1 B and pass through the next A. Don't skip a bead. Peyote 3 with B. Repeat from * four more times. Step up (**figure 12**).

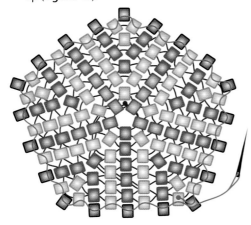

figure 12

Sew on the eyes, nose, and mouth.

Front Layer—Ears

Prepare 1 yard (about 1 m) of thread in your needle as before.

Row 1: String 3 Bs and form a ring secured with a lark's head knot as before. Don't allow the knot to slip into a bead.

Row 2: *Add 2 As and pass through the next B . Repeat from * two more times. Step up (**figure 13**).

figure 13

Note: These beads form the three corners of the triangle. Make sure the pairs of beads at each corner sit almost parallel to each other. Adjust them if necessary.

Row 3: *Add 2 Bs and pass through the next A. Add 1 B, skip one bead in the row below, and pass through the next A. Repeat from * two more times. Step up (**figure 14**).

figure 14

Row 4: *Add 2 As and pass through the next B. Peyote twice with A. Repeat from * two more times. Step up (**figure 15**).

figure 15

Row 5: Peyote two sides with B. Add only 1 B at each of the three corners (**figure 16**).

figure 16

Zip the third side of the triangle to one side of the domed pentagon (**figure 17**). Weave in the thread and clip.

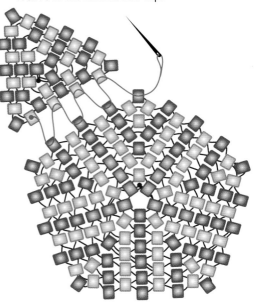

figure 17

Repeat for the second ear.

Back Layer

Make the back layer like the front, following the directions for rows 1–10 of the face.

Assemble

Zip the back to the front, aligning the single corner beads of the front between the two corner beads of the back. Add a loop of beads or a closed ring between the ears if you intend to wear this item as a pendant. Weave in the thread and trim. To stiffen, dip the face in clear acrylic floor polish and allow it to dry.

MOUNTAIN LAUREL PIN

The delicate pink buds of the mountain laurel shrub open into cup-shaped flowers with five connected petals and as many as ten stamens.

SUPPLIES

Size 11° cylinder beads:

A (flowers), 8 g

Size 15° seed beads:

B (flowers), < 1 g

C (flowers), < 1 g

3 size 8° seed beads:

D (flowers)

Size 11° cylinder beads:

E (leaves), 1 g

F (leaves), 2 g

1 perforated beading disk and back plate with pin back, 1 inch (2.5 cm) in diameter

Nymo D or FireLine 6 lb

Size 10 beading needle

Microcrystalline wax

Scissors

Lighter

DIMENSIONS

2½ x 1¾ inches (6.5 x 4.5 cm)

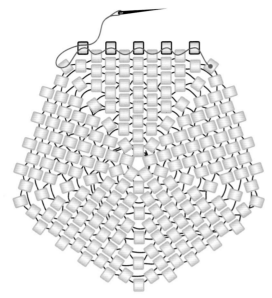

figure 1

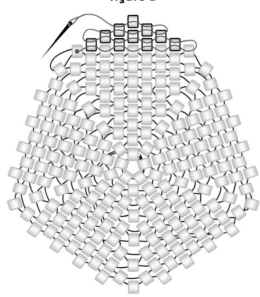

figure 2

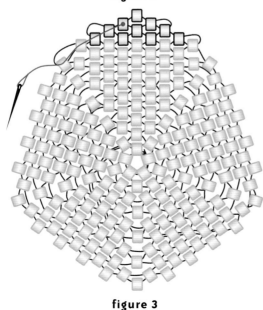

Flowers

With 2 yards (about 2 m) of thread in your needle, bring the ends together, wax well, knot, clip the tail close to the knot, and melt the ends slightly.

Rows 1–11: Follow the directions for rows 1–11 of the Cute Cat (or Dog) Face on page 152, but work with all A beads.

Rows 12–14: Repeat rows 9–11 once.

Rows 15–19: *With your thread exiting a single corner bead, peyote across one side of the pentagon with A until your thread exits the next corner bead. Without adding a bead, turn and pass back through the last bead added in this row (edge decrease). Continue working back and forth until there is one bead left (**figures 1** and **2**). Pass through the edge beads on one side, exiting a single corner bead* (**figure 3**). Repeat from * to * four more times.

After completing the fifth point, weave in the thread and clip.

Stamen

Prepare 1 yard (about 1 m) of thread as before.

Start a new thread at the flower's center. Add 6 Bs and 1 C and pass through any bead above it on rows 9 to 11. Pass back through the beads just added and pass through the nearest A on row 1 or 2. Repeat this step nine more times, positioning the stamen as in the photo below. Stitch 1 D to the flower's center. Weave in the thread and clip. Set aside and repeat these steps to make two more flowers.

figure 3

Leaves

The leaves are made with single-layer pointed ovals. With 2 yards (about 2 m) of thread in your needle, bring the ends together, wax well, knot, clip the tail close to the knot, and melt the ends slightly.

Row 1: String 1 E, 9 Fs, 4 Es, 9 Fs, and 3 Es and form a ring secured with a lark's head knot as follows: Push the beads to within 1 inch (2.5 cm) of the knot. Separate the strands between the beads and the knot. Pass the needle between the strands, tighten, then pass back through the last bead strung (**figures 4** and **5**). Don't allow the knot to slip into a bead. Orient the work so you're working counterclockwise (lefties, work clockwise).

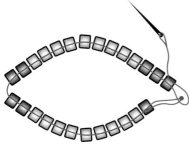

figure 4

figure 5

Row 2: *Add 2 Es and pass through the next E. Don't skip a bead (**figure 6**). Peyote the side with F. Repeat from * once. Step up (**figure 7**).

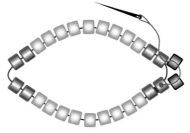

figure 6

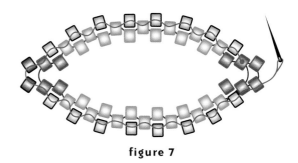

figure 7

Row 3: *Add 2 Es and pass through the next E. Don't skip a bead. Peyote the side with F. Repeat from * once. Step up.

Row 4: *Add 1 E and pass through the next E. Don't skip a bead. Peyote the side with F. Repeat from * once. Step up. Don't tighten the thread. Set the needle and thread aside.

Repeat this step twice for a total of three leaves. Vary the size of the leaves by adding 2 Fs to each side when you string the beads in row 1.

Assemble

Stitch the three leaves to the perforated plate. Stitch the flowers over the leaves so the petals touch. Attach the perforated plate to the back plate.

SUPPLIES

Size 11° cylinder beads:

A (shown in dark gray), 2 g

B (shown in red), 7 g

68 black 2-mm round crystals (Swarovski 5000), or black size 11° seed beads, 1 g

1 narrow pin back, 1½ inches (3.8 cm)

1 large paper clip, 1⅞ inches (4.75 cm)

FireLine 6 lb

Size 10 beading needle

Microcrystalline wax

Scissors

Lighter

Flat-nose pliers

Round-nose pliers

DIMENSIONS

2¼ inches (5.5 cm) on each side

SPIRAL TRIANGLE PIN

This pin is made using flat peyote stitch with increases at certain intervals to create the triangular shape. Once the first layer is complete, work a second layer starting from the first row of beads. Place an armature between the layers and sew on a pin back. Zip the layers together and embellish the outer edge.

With 3 yards (about 3 m) of thread in your needle, bring the ends together, wax well, knot, clip the tail close to the knot, and melt the ends slightly. Control the thread tension to keep the sides straight. Later, the wire will maintain the pin's shape.

First Layer

Row 1: String a stopper bead, then add 33 Bs, 1 A, 25 Bs, 1 A, 17 Bs, 1 A, 9 Bs, 1 A, and 6 Bs.

Row 2: Add 1 B and pass back through the second-to-last bead. Continue in peyote across the row, adding 2 As above each A. At the end of the row, remove the stopper bead and knot the working thread to the tail (**figure 1**). Turn, and without adding a bead, pass back through the last bead added.

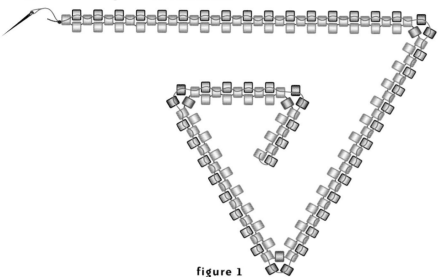

figure 1

flat-nose pliers, then bend it as shown in **figure 2**, using round-nose pliers.

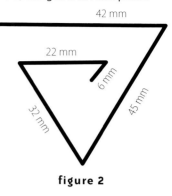

42 mm

22 mm

6 mm

32 mm

45 mm

figure 2

Place the armature between the two layers. Zip the second layer to the first. Sew the 2-mm round crystals or seed beads to the spiral triangle, stitching in the ditch along the outer edge.

Rows 3–7: Peyote across the row, adding 2 As between the 2 As at each corner. At the end of each row, turn, and without adding a bead, pass back through the last bead added. You will now have six pairs of A beads at each corner.

Row 8: Repeat row 2, but add only 1 A between the 2 As at each corner.

Weave through to the first row and exit the first bead strung.

Second Layer

Row 1: Peyote across the row, passing through the single A at each corner.

Rows 2–6: Add 1 B and pass through the second-to-last bead. Continue in peyote across the row, adding 2 As above each A. At the end of each row, turn, and without adding a bead, pass back through the last bead added.

Sew the pin back to the outside of the second layer.

Assemble

To help the beadwork hold its shape, place a wire armature between the two layers before zipping. To make the armature, straighten a large paper clip with

Variations

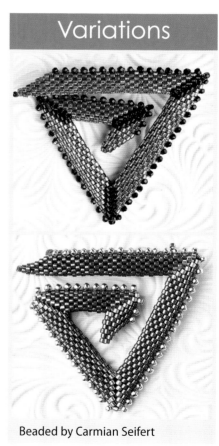

Beaded by Carmian Seifert

Size 11° cylinder beads:

A (shown in dark gray), 2 g

B (shown in light gray), 12 g

113 black 6-mm crystal bicones
(Swarovski 5328)

27 black 4-mm crystal bicones
(Swarovski 5328)

42 black 2-mm round crystals
(Swarovski 5000)

4 gold 5-mm rondelles

1 black 5-mm round crystal
(Swarovski 5000)

3 black 10 x 6-mm fire-polished drops

Single-strand clasp

FireLine 6 lb

Size 10 beading needle

Microcrystalline wax

Scissors

Lighter

DIMENSIONS

22 inches (56 cm)

PENTAGONS AND CRYSTALS NECKLACE

**The simple pentagon shape with radiating crystal centers
becomes an elegant necklace.**

Pentagons

With 1 yard (about 1 m) of thread in the needle, bring the ends together, wax well, knot, clip the tail close to the knot, and melt the ends slightly.

Row 1: String 5 Bs and form a ring secured with a lark's head knot as follows: Push the beads to within 1 inch (2.5 cm) of the knot. Separate the strands between the beads and the knot. Pass the needle between the strands, tighten, then pass back through the last bead strung (**figures 1** and **2**). Don't allow the knot to slip into a bead. Orient the work so you're working counterclockwise (lefties, work clockwise).

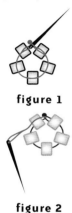

figure 1

figure 2

Row 2: *Add one 6-mm crystal and 1 A. Pass back through the crystal and pass through the next bead on the ring. Repeat from * four more times. Step up through the first crystal and the A (**figure 3**).

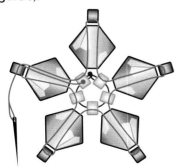

figure 3

Row 3: Add 7 Bs and pass through the next A. Repeat from * four more times. Step up (**figure 4**).

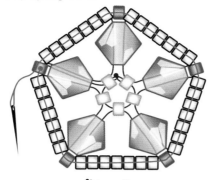

figure 4

Row 4: *Peyote 4 with B and pass through the single corner A beads. Repeat from * four more times. Step up (**figure 5**). You'll have four "up" beads on each side.

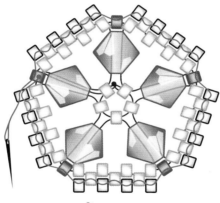

figure 5

Row 5: *Peyote 3 with B. Add 2 As above the A at the corner. Repeat from * four more times. Step up (**figure 6**).

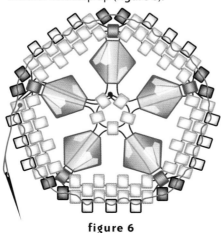

figure 6

Row 6: Peyote 3 with B. *Add 1 A between the 2 As at the next corner. Peyote 4 with B. Repeat from * 3 times, then add 1 A between the 2 As at the next corner and peyote once with B. Step up (**figure 7**). Leave the thread attached to connect the pentagons or connect the pentagons as you complete them (see next page). Set aside and repeat to make a total of 19 pentagons.

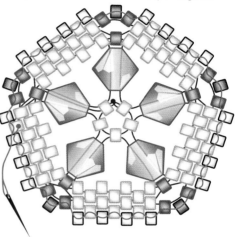

figure 7

Assemble

Weave through beads and exit a corner of a pentagon. Add one 6-mm bicone crystal, pass through a corner bead on the next pentagon, then pass back through the crystal and the corner bead of the pentagon just exited. Repeat to reinforce (**figure 8**).

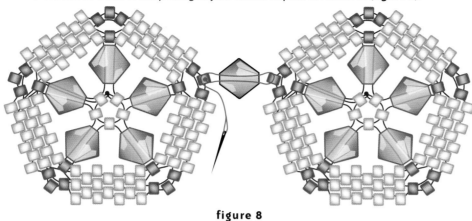

figure 8

Connect two sets of nine pentagons in this manner. Add one 6-mm bicone crystal and half the clasp to the first pentagon of each set. Connect the two sets with a 4-mm bicone. This becomes the center of the necklace (**figure 9**).

figure 9

Weave through to the next lower corner of the left pentagon, add one 2-mm crystal, and pass through a corner of the remaining pentagon. (This becomes the center bottom pentagon.) Add one 2-mm crystal and pass through the lower corner of the pentagon on the right. Add one 2-mm crystal and pass through the corner of the left pentagon. Repeat to reinforce the thread path. These three 2-mm crystals form a triangle in the center.

Weave through to the outer lower corner of the left pentagon and connect it to the outer corner of the center bottom pentagon with a 4-mm bicone crystal as shown in **figure 9**. Weave through beads and repeat on the other side or attach a new thread to connect the right pentagon with the center bottom pentagon.

Tassel

Anchor your thread so it exits a corner bead on the center bottom pentagon as shown in **figure 9**. Add seven 2-mm crystals, 1 rondelle, the 5-mm round crystal, ten 2-mm crystals, 1 rondelle, 1 drop, and 1 A. Skip the A and pass back through the drop, rondelle, 2-mm crystals, round crystal, and rondelle.

Make a half-hitch knot between beads (**figure 10**). Pass back through the rondelle and the 5-mm round crystal. Add the second strand of fringe in a similar manner, but add only nine 2-mm crystals on the lower part of the strand. Repeat for the third strand using six 2-mm crystals.

figure 10

After completing the third strand and exiting the rondelle above the round crystal, add seven 2-mm crystals and pass through the right corner of the center bottom pentagon. Weave in the thread and clip.

Variations

Beaded by Doris Coghill

Quick Guide to the Four Basic Shapes

Once you're familiar with the four basic shapes in this book—triangles, squares, pentagons, and hexagons—use this quick reference as a refresher. Here, A beads form the corners; B beads, the sides. Start each shape with a ring of beads secured with a lark's head knot. Step up at the end of every row except the last.

Triangle (three sides)

Row 1: String 3 As and form a ring secured with a lark's head knot. Pass back through the last bead strung.

Row 2: *Add 2 As and pass through the next bead. Repeat from * twice.

Row 3: *Add 2 As and pass through the next A. Peyote the side with B. Repeat from * twice.

Repeat: Continue stitching row 3 until your triangle is the desired size.

Final row (optional): Add 1 A at each corner.

Square (four sides)

Row 1: String 4 As and form a ring secured with a lark's head knot. Pass back through the last bead strung.

Row 2: *Add 1 B and pass through the next A. Repeat from * 3 more times.

Row 3: Add 3 As at each corner. Push the center bead down so it touches the bead in the row below.

Row 4: Add 2 As at each corner as follows: after exiting the first A of the

3 As added in the previous row, add 2 As and pass through the third A. Peyote the sides with B.

Row 5: Add 2 As at each corner. Peyote the sides with B.

Row 6: Add 1 A between the 2 As at each corner. Peyote the sides with B.

Row 7: Peyote around with B.

Repeat: Continue stitching rows 3–7 until your square is the desired size. End with row 6.

Pentagon (five sides)

Row 1: String 5 As and form a ring secured with a lark's head knot. Pass back through the last bead strung.

Row 2: *Add 1 B and pass through the next bead. Repeat from * 4 more times.

Row 3: *Add 2 As and pass through the next bead. Repeat from * 4 more times. (These pairs form the V at each corner.)

Row 4: Peyote around with B, adding 1 A between the pair of beads at each corner.

Row 5: Peyote around with B.

Row 6: Add 3 As at each corner. Push the center bead down so it touches the bead in the row below. Peyote the sides with B.

Row 7: Add 2 As at each corner as follows: After exiting the first A of the 3 As added in the previous row, add 2 As and pass through the third A. Peyote the sides with B.

Repeat: Continue stitching rows 4–7 until your pentagon is the desired size. End with row 4.

Hexagon (six sides)

Row 1: String 6 Bs and form a ring secured with a lark's head knot. Pass back through the last bead strung.

Row 2: *Add 1 A and pass through the next bead. Repeat from * 5 more times.

Row 3: Peyote around with B.

Row 4: *Add 2 As and pass through the next B. Repeat from * 5 more times.

Row 5: Add 1 A between the 2 As at each corner. Peyote the sides with B.

Row 6: Peyote around with B.

Row 7: Add 2 As above the single A at each corner. Peyote the sides with B.

Repeat: Continue stitching rows 5–7 until your hexagon is the desired size. End with row 5.

Quick Reference

For more information about shapes, including their names and wireframe diagrams, go to www.mathworld.com. You can also learn more about the five Platonic solids, the 13 Archimedean solids, and the 81 Johnson solids, many of which can be constructed in beadwork using these four basic shapes.

Any of the basic shapes can be joined to one another if they both have the same number of beads on the sides and a single bead at the corner of the last row. For example, the side of a five-row triangle can be joined to the side of a six-row square by adding connector beads (an extra row of beads) to either side. Similarly, the sides of a six-row square can be joined to the side of an eight-row pentagon or the side of an 11-row hexagon.

To make domed shapes, use the increase pattern for one shape but make the shape with fewer sides. For example, for a low dome, use the hexagon increase pattern (2, 1, 0), but make it with only five beads in the beginning ring and five sides. For a steeper dome, use the pentagon increase pattern (3, 2, 1, 0 at the corners), but start with only four beads in the beginning ring and four sides.

For more distorted shapes, use the triangle increase pattern (2, 2, 2), but start with five beads in the beginning ring and five sides.

The more you experiment with shapes, the more intrigued you'll be!

Quick Reference

Triangle

Row	Corners	Sides
1	3*	-
2	2	0
3	2	1
4	2	2
5	2	3
6	2	4
7	2	5
8	2	6
9	2	7
10	2	8

Square

Row	Corners	Sides
1	4*	-
2	0	1
3	3	0
4	2	1
5	2	2
6	1	3
7	0	4
8	3	3
9	2	4
10	2	5
11	1	6

Pentagon

Row	Corners	Sides
1	5*	-
2	0	1
3	2	0
4	1	1
5	0	2
6	3	1
7	2	2
8	1	3
9	0	3
10	3	3
11	2	4
12	1	5

Hexagon

Row	Corners	Sides
1	6*	-
2	6	0
3	0	1
4	2	0
5	1	1
6	0	2
7	2	1
8	1	2
9	0	3
10	2	2
11	1	3

* This is the number of beads in the beginning ring.

Connecting Shapes

The four basic shapes shown here have three "up" beads on each side and a single bead at each corner. They can be zipped together easily by adding a row of connector beads between them.

TRIANGLE ROW 5

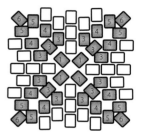

SQUARE ROW 6

PENTAGON ROW 8

HEXAGON ROW 11

Chart Your Own Patterns

Use the grids on this page and the next three to chart patterns for the four basic shapes used in this book.

You have permission to photocopy these grids.

TRIANGLE GRID FOR CYLINDER BEADS

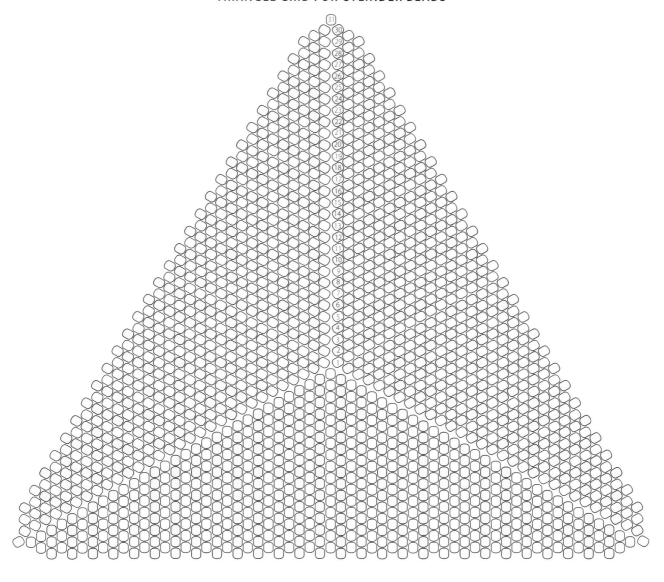

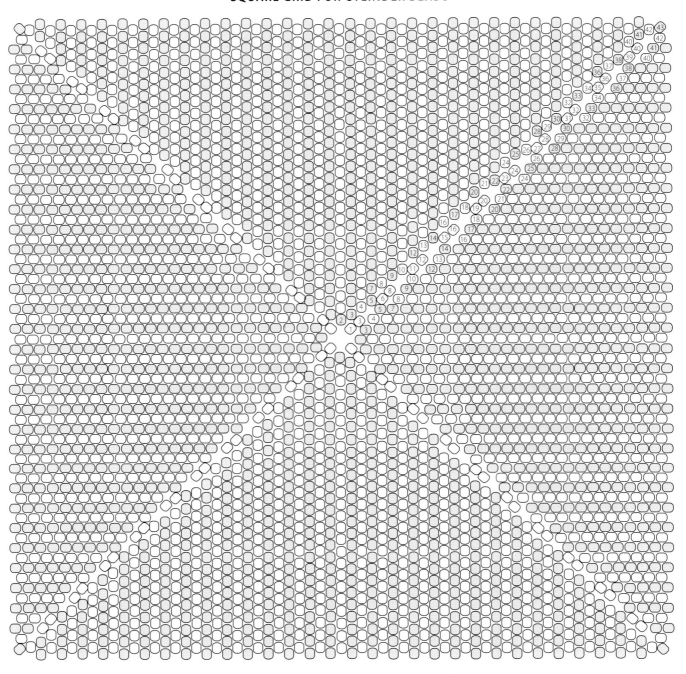

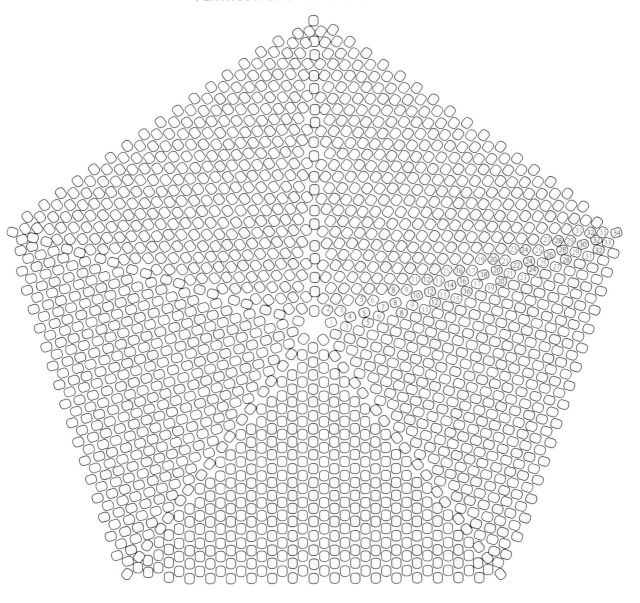

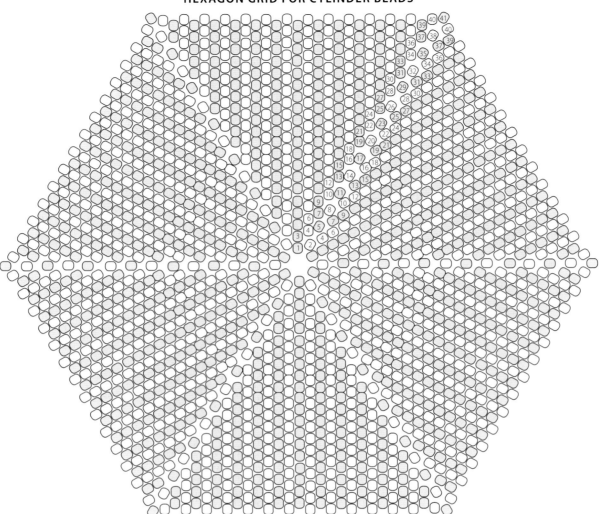

Gallery

A SEANA BETTENCOURT
Untitled, 2013
21 x 2 x 1 cm
Seed beads, silver-plated beads, thread;
peyote stitch
Photo by Shannon Bettencourt

B JENNY BOYLE
Iceni Torque, 2011
15.5 x 15 cm
Seed beads, cylinder beads, freshwater
pearls, rivolis, nailheads, wire armature;
peyote stitch, netting, off-loom beadweaving
Photo by Ross Paxton

C DIANE FITZGERALD
Hexagon Bracelet, 2011
10 x 10 x 1.5 cm
Seed beads; peyote stitch
Photo by artist

D SANDY HOUK
Rococo, 2008
50 cm long
Seed beads, crystals, thread; peyote stitch
Photo by Lynne Harty

A

B

Top view

C

A This piece evolved from the Trillium Flowers in the book *Diane Fitzgerald's Shaped Beadwork*. It was made by adding more increases on the sides between the first mid-side increase and the corner.

DIANE FITZGERALD
Ode to Mandelbrot, 2011
Focal element, 7.6 cm across at top
Miyuki Delica beads, Nymo D thread, glass teardrop beads
Photo by Lynne Harty

B JUDITH GOLAN
Time for Teapots, 2008
4.5 x 6 x 3.5 cm
Seed beads, beading thread; peyote stitch, square stitch, tubular peyote stitch
Photo by artist

C DANA CLEAK
Flame Goblet, 2012
Cup, 4.2 x 8 cm
Seed beads, drop beads, round faceted crystals, bicones, rivolis, thread
Photos by Heather Nelson

Bottom

D DANA CLEAK
Floral Truffle Case, 2011
7 cm in diameter
Seed beads, bicones, acrylic glass flowers,
thread; peyote stitch, odd-count peyote
stitch, tubular peyote stitch, embellishment
Photos by Diane Fitzgerald

E MARY REITHMEIER
Vintage Elegance, 2011
30 x 7 x 1 cm
Cylinder beads, antique black beads, glass
spacers, glass drop, thread; peyote stitch,
herringbone chain
Photo by Pitkin Studio

A DIANE FITZGERALD
Four Tiny Teapots, 2009
Largest, 6 x 5 x 5 cm
Seed beads; peyote stitch
Photo by Lynne Harty

B MARY REITHMEIER
Gail's Garden, 2012
28 x 9 x 1.5 cm
Cylinder beads, seed beads,
bugle beads, rose montees, small
crystals, thread; peyote stitch
Photo by Pitkin Studio

C CARMEN FALB
Juggling Colors, 2010
30 x 6 x 3 cm
Seed beads, crystals, thread;
peyote stitch
Photo by Lynne Harty

D MARY LOU ALLEN
Untitled, 2008
25 x 18 x 3 cm
Cylinder beads, round seed beads, metal beads, metal
findings, thread, wire; peyote stitch, herringbone
stitch, stringing
Photo by Diane Fitzgerald

E NINA C. DILLMAN
Sweetheart Earrings, 2011
Heart, 3 x 4 cm
Seed beads, pearls, findings, thread; peyote stitch
Photo by artist

F This is Suzanne Golden's oversized version
of the Oh My Stars! Necklace on page 18.

SUZANNE GOLDEN
Star Power Necklace, 2009
73.7 cm long
Large black and white seed beads, vintage black and
white striped beads, red ceramic disk beads
Photo by artist

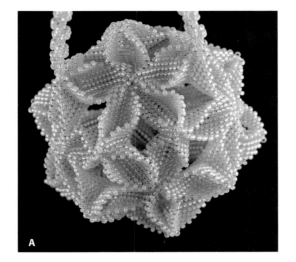

A SAVITA PERSIC
Trillium Globe, 2011
10 x 10 x 10 cm
20 beaded trilliums, seed beads; peyote stitch
Photo by Graham F. Teixeira

B MARY LOU ALLEN
Deco Scarab, 2006
35 x 13 x 2 cm
Cylinder beads, metal buttons, rhinestone, scarab, wood dowels, dagger beads; peyote stitch, herringbone stitch
Photo by Diane Fitzgerald

C DIANE FITZGERALD
Multi-Color Beaded Bead Necklace, 2010
Each smaller bead, 3 x 3 x 3 cm
Seed beads; peyote stitch
Photo by artist

Credits

Editor
Nathalie Mornu

Technical Editor
Mindy Brooks

Editorial Assistance
Dawn Dillingham
Hannah Doyle

Art Director & Cover Designer
Kathleen Holmes

Illustrator
Melissa Grakowsky Shippee

Photographer
Lynne Harty

The gold and black earrings on the front cover were beaded by Ann Gilbert.

About the Author

After raising two children, gaining a graduate degree in mass communications, and working in the electric utility industry, Diane Fitzgerald changed course for a full-time career in beads and has never looked back.

Diane's passion for beads began when she was about 10 years old, with the Christmas gift of a Walco bead loom kit. The feel of the beads, their colors, and the rhythm of weaving all clicked with her. Later, as an adult, she learned more beading from notables such as Horace Goodhue, Carol Perrenoud, Virginia Blakelock, and Helen Banes. With the basics well in hand, she began designing jewelry with beads and writing and illustrating instructions for teaching and publication.

Beads have led her on a journey of learning and travel from Alaska to South Africa, from England to Japan, with many stops in between. For her, though, it is the lasting friendships that have made each stop memorable.

In 2008, Diane was invited to join the original group of Swarovski Ambassadors, and a new world of friends and crystals opened to her.

This volume marks an even dozen books authored by Diane. Each presents unique material documenting her exploration of beadwork and her desire to pass along not only her designs but also her pleasure in beading.

Acknowledgments

Among the many people who put their shoulder to the wheel to bring this book about, I would like to thank in particular two very special individuals, Mindy Brooks, the technical editor, and Nathalie Mornu, the editor. Both exhibited dedication, perseverance, and patience beyond the call of duty. Special thanks also to Melissa Grakowsky Shippee, the illustrator; Lynne Harty, the photographer; and Kathleen Holmes, the art director. I am deeply indebted to them and to all the staff at Lark who brought this book into being.

Special thanks to my loyal friends, the Beadheads Superstars: Carla Abler-Erickson, Doris Coghill, Ann Gilbert, Jane Langenback, Liana Magee, Susan Manchester, Sonya Monzel, Carmian Seifert, and Peggy Wright for their help, their friendship and the joy they bring to beading; to Kenji Katsuoka at MIYUKI Company of Japan, who has supported me in so many ways; to Rusty Cole at E. H. Ashley Company, who promptly and cheerfully answers all my questions about Swarovski Crystal Elements; to the Swarovski Company for its support through the Create Your Style Ambassador program of which I am a member; and to all my students near and far, my warmest thanks and appreciation.

also by
DIANE FITZGERALD

Index